STRUGGLING
WELL

STRUGGLING WELL

DR. FRED ANTONELLI

CROSSLINK
PUBLISHING

Struggling Well

℘ CrossLink Publishing
℃ www.crosslinkpublishing.com

Copyright, © 2017 Fred Antonelli, Ph.D.

ISBN 978-1-63357-105-1

Library of Congress Control Number: 2017934112

Unless otherwise indicated, scripture quotations are taken from THE HOLY BIBLE, NEW INTERNATIONAL VERSION®, NIV® Copyright © 1973, 1978, 1984, 2011 by Biblica, Inc.™ Used by permission. All rights reserved worldwide.

Scripture quotations marked (NLT) are taken from the Holy Bible, New Living Translation, copyright © 1996, 2004, 2007 by Tyndale House Foundation. Used by permission of Tyndale House Publishers, Inc., Carol Stream, IL 60188. All rights reserved.

Scripture quotations marked "MSG" are taken from *The Message*. Copyright © 1993, 1994, 1996, 2000, 2001, 2002. Used by permission of NavPress Publishing Group.

Scripture quotations marked NKJV are taken from the New King James Version®. Copyright 1982 by Thomas Nelson, Inc. Used by permission. All rights reserved.

Scripture quotations marked "NASB" are taken from the NEW AMERICAN STANDARD BIBLE®, Copyright © 1960, 1962, 1963, 1968, 1971, 1972, 1973, 1975, 1977, 1995 by The Lockman Foundation. Used by permission.

Scripture quotations marked "Phillips" are taken from The New Testament in Modern English, copyright © 1958, 1959, 1960 J.B. Phillips and 1947, 1952, 1955, 1957 The Macmillian Company, New York. Used by permission. All rights reserved.

"One of the saddest situations I encounter is when someone collapses into their problem and ends up in a hopeless and helpless state. At least they believe that to be true. A painful life experience wasted rather than it being the beginning of a whole new life of meaning, purpose, and fulfillment that can happen when God is in control and the struggler is connected with redemptive relationships. *Struggling Well* is an effective guide to a path of healing, restoration, and strength. As a fellow struggler, I wish I had read this book forty years ago. Dr. Antonelli is an excellent communicator and I truly believe this book will help thousands find their way to a redemptive path out of their painful struggle, and into a life of the promises and awareness of God's wonderful grace and unconditional love."

Steve Arterburn, New Life Ministries,
Host of New Life Live

"In his book *Struggling Well*, Dr. Fred Antonelli releases a fresh aroma of the grace of God. With a deep commitment to the ageless principles of the Bible and a genuine scriptural compassion, life's conflicts find purpose and meaning. From the Psalms of David to the ministry of Jesus, the common thread is a cry for love and acceptance. This book weaves together our fallen nature and God's forgiveness to make us a truly new person. A must for the pulpit and the pew."

Rev. Paul Johansson, President Emeritus,
Elim Bible Institute and College

"Decades ago segments of the church so emphasized supernatural physical healing that they forbade worshippers from going to a doctor for treatment. Now we understand that God sometimes uses medical doctors to heal us. I believe we are in a similar transition now with mental health. The solution to my personal struggle that resulted in my 2006 scandal was trauma resolution therapy. God used mental health professionals to answer my prayers.

Dr. Fred Antonelli's book, *Struggling Well*, is a must-read for every modern Bible believer. This book includes vital information that every competent Christian leader needs. If those who had no idea what to do to help me and my family in 2006 would have had this book, our story would have modeled the healing power of the church much more powerfully."

Ted Haggard, Sr. Pastor, St. James Church,
Colorado Springs, CO

Struggling Well is the next level of understanding our journey with Christ. Pivotal. Relational. Practical. Through the heart of a pastor and counselor, Dr. Fred Antonelli leads us into an unfiltered authentic relationship with God to discover the freedom of true life. Every pastor, church staff member, and Christian should embrace this book so you no longer struggle alone.

Wade Haskins - Lead Pastor, Way of Life Community
Church, Bel Air, MD

"Provocative. Gracious. Insightful. Thoughtful. *Struggling Well* may challenge some of your life doctrines, fill in the blanks for other restorative paradigms, and ultimately deliver a great value to your life. This book is powerful for those in recovery from pain, as well as those supporting others in recovery. Drawing from his extensive experience as a pastor, psychologist and therapist, Dr. Fred Antonelli brings a wealth of proven tools to help the hurting. I hope everyone will take advantage of this great gift!"

Patrick Norris, Sr. Pastor, LifePointe Church,
Kansas City, KS

TABLE OF CONTENTS

DR. FRED ANTONELLI

FOREWORD

He's heard it all + seen it all

You will find no condemnation here. But you will find acknowledgement and understanding of our human condition. Dr. Fred is not shockable. He has heard it all and gives well-reasoned, thoughtful, gentle and sometimes not so gentle understanding of ourselves. He doesn't offer excuses, but gives us a deeper appreciation of how we respond to our unpredictable journey of life—the struggle. He brings understanding as a psychologist and theologian—a great combination!

This book will lift the condemnation others—or yourself—have heaped upon you causing you to build a protective wall that has shut others out—including God. You are living isolated and alone. You're just trying to survive.

Dr. Fred understands us. He is one of us! Therefore, he doesn't talk down to us from some ivory tower but struggles with us against our defeat, discouragement, and dysfunction to lift our eyes from our mess to God's purpose for us. He unlocks our condemning, negative attitudes about ourselves that bind us in defeat and repetitive failure. He explains in a way we can understand that God has so much more for us. He puts the hay down where the cows can reach it! Sometimes he is shocking. Sometimes he is irreverent. All the time he is honest. More times than not he will express what you are feeling and didn't know how to put it into words.

Dr. Fred Antonelli has been talking and listening for years to wounded, battered believers struggling with their "human condition." In this book, he gives thoughtful insight, powerful understanding, and balanced wisdom that enable us to understand who we are— flawed but redeemed sinners deeply loved by God.

Ruth Graham

failure was never accepted in the home or church. Parents need to allow children to fail to learn that this is _normal_, _acceptable_, and that ALL of us make mistakes and that there are consequences. However, children need _not_ _fear failure_.

PREFACE

In the fall of 2009, I was sitting outside eating at a seafood restaurant in St. Michaels, Maryland, on the Miles River with a good friend of mine, Ed Gungor. Ed is senior pastor of Sanctuary Church in Tulsa, Oklahoma, bishop in the Communion of Evangelical Episcopal Churches, a New York Times best-selling author, and a brilliant thinker. He had come to look over our counseling practice, specifically our sexual addiction three-day intensive program here on the Eastern Shore of Maryland. He was looking for a good clinical/Christian program to recommend to not only his parishioners, but other pastors as well.

As we sat there eating and enjoying conversation (something that Italians like me love to do) I began sharing with Ed about the hot topic of mental health issues in the church today. Within the evangelical church, when you mention the term "mental health issues," in particular within the Charismatic branch of the church, it's often looked at as a *theological stigma* rather than a reality. I remember saying, "Ed, people in the church are struggling with mental health issues, and they feel isolated and even ashamed in their church to talk about their challenge." Ed responded with something hugely profound to me. He said, "Fred, we all struggle, every one of us, and both the leadership in the church as well as the sheep need to know that, and though we struggle, we can all *struggle well.*"

Ed blew my mind! It was like God rushed through my brain like a whirlwind and made crystal clear what I had been trying to say for years regarding the subject of mental health issues in the church. After I settled down, I said, "Ed, can I take that phrase you just said, "*struggle well*," and use it for a book that I've wanted to write?" He said, "Sure, it's yours." It was a "title" that I had been looking for and I finally found it thanks to the Holy Spirit using my friend. Funny, that's how I've been all of my ministry as a former pastor and even when I speak today. I have to have "a title" before I can build a sermon. I have stuff in my head, but it's the *title* that sets the sermon in motion, not the reverse.

The struggling soul of man is as old as Adam and as recent as each morning when you wake up and face your day. It was Job who said, "*Is not all human life a struggle?* (Job 7:1). The question isn't whether we struggle in life ... we do. The real question is why do we struggle, and through the struggle is it possible for us, as Ed Gungor suggested, to *struggle well*?

This book is written to every soul that has found life's unscripted surprises both challenging and even painful. It's for the person looking for healthy ways to navigate around the questions, disappointments, and pitfalls of this earthly experience. It's these types of encounters in life that cause us to scratch our head, then renavigate and go a different direction ... at times a direction that leads through a vale of tears, disbelief, sorrow, and even regret.

But to be more specific, this book is a labor of love to all of my spiritually weary evangelical clients, friends, and church leaders, those who found themselves, like the unfortunate man in the parable of the Good Samaritan: "*stripped [of] his clothes, beaten up, and left half dead beside the road.*" They desperately longed for a compassionate helper to pour "*oil and wine*" on their wounds and provide a bandage, but as much as they looked, they couldn't find anyone. Instead of a Good Samaritan, more often they found unsympathetic, pharisaic, well-meaning people who just couldn't understand why the suffering ones "didn't have enough faith" to get through their struggle. Yes, the suffering ones: those who felt abandoned, alone, and spiritually confused as 'they tried to balance their pain and questions against God's love and truth. Followers of Jesus hurt so deeply they would rather entrust their theologically forbidden questions, their failures, and their emotional pain to a professional therapist rather than their own pastor or denominational leader. It's the rejection and spiritual isolation that they fear from their fellow believers. And then after praying 10,000 prayers in 10,000 different ways, and still not receiving help in their struggle, they come to the sad conclusion that God must have abandoned them as well.

You might say, "Fred, aren't you being overly dramatic here?" To that I would say absolutely not. From my experience and perspective as a former senior pastor and a licensed mental health professional, I have seen this mentality in the church and much more when counseling individuals and couples throughout the years. It's not that "the church" is being deliberately cruel when it comes to theological heavy-handedness. It's just that where there is a pervasive legalistic mentality, there's also the presence of an unempathetic heart. Jesus feels our pain because He Himself experienced pain emotionally, physically, and yes, spiritually. And it was out of this human pain that He became familiar with our human struggle. It was because *"He was a man of sorrows [and] acquainted with deepest grief,"* that He could connect with us through empathy and compassion. And it was out of His painful struggle to recapture our souls that He came to understand what they go through.

Someone said, *"Once you finally make it to the point of making it, it's only then will you appreciate the struggle."* God paid a very large and costly price with the blood of His Son for all of us to be able to "make it," yes, while in these frail, broken clay bodies.

Most believers have, are, or will walk in a dichotomous relationship with God. It's the world of hope and faith versus the world of doubt and questions. The two collide with each other, and for sure they did with King David. Look at Psalm 13.

O Lord, how long will you forget me? Forever?
How long will you look the other way?
2 How long must I struggle with anguish in my soul,
with sorrow in my heart every day?
How long will my enemy have the upper hand?
3 Turn and answer me, O Lord my God!
Restore the sparkle to my eyes, or I will die.
4 Don't let my enemies gloat, saying, "We have defeated him!"
Don't let them rejoice at my downfall.

Then in the same breath, as if David were bipolar, there's verses 5–6.

5 But I trust in your unfailing love.
I will rejoice because you have rescued me.
6 I will sing to the Lord
because he is good to me.

This didn't make David unspiritual or even unfaithful to God. It just made him human. This is the thing I find that we evangelicals struggle with so much in our faith walk, being theologically honest regarding our fallen human condition. We need to know that we can mess up, fall short, suffer with depression, anxiety, doubts, fears, make mistakes (sometimes big ones) and still say at the end of the day, *"I will trust in your unfailing love. I will rejoice because you have rescued me."* When David said, *"How long must I struggle with anguish in my soul?"* it was a man crying out from his human condition, not a person being seen by God as weak or less than. This is not how God sees us in our struggle. His love, compassion, mercy, and grace are much larger than our evangelically minded prejudices.

My hope and prayer for the reader is that in some way this book speaks to your struggling heart as much as it does mine. It's true that no one fits into a cookie-cutter mold, so not everything in this book will apply to all people. However, I do believe within these pages there will be something that can be helpful to you as you're walking through your life's journey, something that will say to you, "Yes, my Christian life has not been void of struggle, but at least now I know that I can *struggle well*."

Fred Antonelli, Ph.D.

ACKNOWLEDGEMENTS

To my wife Debbie, for your endless unconditional love,
devotion and tolerance through the many hours and time
denied you as I plowed through this book.
You will forever be my constant stable in life.
What would I do without you?

To Ed Gungor, for making yourself available to the Holy
Spirit in expressing a phrase that gave me a platform to
build this book on. Thank you for your friendship, passion,
empathetic heart and pastoral soul care.

To Ted and Gayle Haggard, for not giving in or giving
up through the intense onslaught of evangelical legalism
during your darkest days. Your endurance has shown us all
what it means to *struggle well*.

To Bill and Peg Hosker, for opening your beautiful
waterfront Chesapeake home to me on multiple occasions
so I could write while basking in nautical serenity.
Your love, care, friendship, and selfless giving showed
me what Jesus looks like.

And finally to my many beloved clients who, if it weren't for you entrusting me with your "dark night of the soul," I would have little to say and even less to give.
I am endlessly humbled.
All of you are my biggest heroes.

INTRODUCTION

It was a summer night in our little Pentecostal church when the missionary-evangelist made the strongest appeal I had ever heard for a no-holds-barred, no-nonsense commitment to Jesus Christ. I had been in dozens of those altar calls before and had responded to them all. But this night carried an urgency that was palpable.

"This is what our young people need," the evangelist said in earnest, nearly in tears. "Commitment!!"

He's right, I thought. *If I could just pull off what he was asking of us. Maybe I could cross that line to real transformation* ("sanctification" was the term we liked to use to imagine a life free from besetting sin). So, I joined the herd of young people and headed down to the altar to do business with God. Though I had spent hundreds of hours at altars just like this one, I was trying to hit the mother of all commitments—the commitment of commitments that would keep me consistently holy.

It was like I wanted God to bite me. Kind of like the spider that crossed the path of a radioactive beam and landed on Peter Parker's hand and bit him. Peter, dizzied, collapsed to the floor, and got up as ... *Spider-Man*.

That's what I wanted God to do to me.

I wanted Him to land on me at the altar and bite my soul in a way that would make me fall down and get back up ... *Godly-Man*.

I wanted my opening song each day to be: *"Godly-Man, Godly-Man, does whatever a Godly-Man can."* And I wanted the transformation to be so pervasive and so permanent that even if God died, I'd still be godly.

But as I knelt at that old familiar altar that hot summer night, I felt nothing. No passion. No tears. No magic. I had just heard in no uncertain terms that commitment was essential to Christian holiness—and I realized I was *commitment-challenged*. I was never going to pull off the commitment necessary to be godly. I felt dead. Lost.

But at that dark moment, surprisingly, a verse came to mind. It was something Jesus said: *"If a man remains in me and I in him, he will bear much fruit; apart from me you can do nothing"* (John 15:5).

A light came on.

This verse was saying that being fruitless—or doing "nothing"—is *par* for a human being (apart from Jesus). In other words, "nothing" is the only thing God expects from fallen people who haven't yet learned how to rely on the grace of God. Dr. Fred says it so well in this writing, "Being broken isn't something to be ashamed of. It doesn't minimize you or make you a failure. Actually it confirms both your natural susceptibility to life's pain as well as your total dependency on Him who is able to bring life out of death."

That night at that altar, it hit me—God had *never* expected me to perform for Him in my own strength—though I had always thought He had.

This was a watershed moment in my thinking about faith. I began to realize that the whole "commitment" thing that I was trying for years to perfect was misdirected. God was really after my commitment to *trust* Him, not my commitment to *perform* for Him. He wanted me to be committed to discovering how trust worked

legalism — Be good on your own strength
perform in your power
no allowance for the supernatural

for a guy like me—with my personality and background. He never
wanted me to jump through hoops for Him or to keep myself out of
patterns of sin. *legalism - be good ... do good*

Faith and discipleship were never supposed to be about committing
to *do good*; it was to be about committing to *God*—the One who does
good things *in us*. We can't produce Christianity. It is supernatural.
A promise at the altar to "be good" means about as much to God as
promising to fly for Him. He knows we can't fly.

STRUGGLING WELL

the reputation was on you the focus on you NOT god

Here's the rub that this book addresses well. Transformation is messy.
It is a daily (if not minute-by-minute) practice of finding "the-spout-
where-grace-comes-out." Grace is not native to us; sin is. We have to
deeply struggle to look beyond ourselves to experience grace. In the
words that follow, Dr. Fred takes us into details of what grace looks
like and how we can access it—not just alone—but in the strength
of community. Grace is really there. It may be metaphysical, but it's
real. It may be rife with struggle, but sin is too. *We understand sin not grace*

I wish grace was a permanent repair. How cool would it be if we
just tasted a tad of grace and we ended up being forever changed?
But it doesn't work that way. Experiencing grace is actually more like
taking a shower. So, any attempts at reducing sin requires frequent
"grace showers in the struggle." In other words, washing ourselves
in His grace...participating by rubbing grace into our lives as we
walk through the dustiness of our struggle.

We cannot change our own nature, but grace will suspend us
above it. The task at hand is to figure out how a person like you,
with your background, your past bumps and bruises, your unique
personality and mindset can best tap into grace. Dr. Fred's *Struggling*

Well is a brilliant work that will help you do just that. And it's jammed not only with the spiritual stuff, but also with the psychological research and experience that helps us understand why holiness is such a challenge for us fallen beings.

This writing will help you.

Enjoy!

Bishop Ed Gungor, OSA

Question

If Satan fell why did God allow Satan to cause humans to fall? Why created more spiritual warfare?

Humans were innocent and pure... Why put the Tree of Knowledge of good and evil in the garden in the first place. Having our eyes opened to evil has caused nothing to humans but heartache, sickness, killings, fear, jealousy, covetousness

No life means no curse
life means curse
I choose no life.

1

A MIND DIVIDED

> *"Beware of no man more than of yourself; we carry our worst enemies within us."*
>
> **-Charles Spurgeon**

In the great poem by Charles Wesley (1707–1788) entitled "Wrestling Jacob," he lays out a very clear picture of life's journey, that of the soul, a human heart struggling between good and evil, God and man, blessing and curse.

Come, O Thou Traveller unknown, Whom still I hold, but cannot see, My company before is gone, And I am left alone with Thee. With Thee all night I mean to stay, And wrestle till the break of day.

Wesley is of course writing here about the wrestling match that went on between Jacob and the angel in Genesis 32. Within Jacob's dilemma, Wesley caught a glimpse of the raw human desperation whereby a man, in this case, was caught between two worlds. His first world was a place of deception, lies, self-indulgence, manipulation, greed, and jealousy. His second, the place where he now found himself alone with God, was a world of fear, anxiety, regret, and self-preservation. Jacob was now in a much different place in his life, the

I choose not to be born—God should understand this rather than have a life of struggle with sin.

19

place of having to make a desperate plea to God for blessing, peace, and deliverance from the wrath of his enraged brother, Esau.

The backstory is Jacob, along with his mother Rebecca, had connived and was successful in stealing Esau's blessing from his father Isaac. You have to understand here that an Old Testament blessing of a father to his sons was a really big deal. It included words of encouragement, details regarding each son's inheritance, and prophetic words concerning the future. It was a high honor to receive a blessing from a father, but to lose a blessing from a father was tantamount to a curse. You can imagine how enraged Esau was when he found out that Jacob had deceived his father and ripped him off of the blessing that was meant for him. Because of this Esau set that out to kill his brother. Now Jacob is on the run from his brother Esau, camped out miles away from home and crying out to God for help as his brother swiftly approaches him.

Things really haven't changed that much in how man struggles with God since that moment in history where Jacob stood by the Jabbok River wrestling with an angel. Jacob came to a crossroads in his life where he had to choose a direction in which he was going to walk.

He had been a divided man as well as now being a desperate man. That's a rough place to be no matter how you break it down.

For the believing sojourner, there will eventually come a time for your own personal "Jabbok," a river where there would be a conflict between two paths, a confluence between two streams, a lonely, dusky place, but yet a place where God dwells with us..., *"though I walk through the valley of the shadow of death,... you are with me..."* (Psalm 23:4).

Be assured that at some point there will arise in all of us a time of personal and spiritual conflict. There is no escaping it. It shatters

Wretched lament, mourn, great turmoil, wrestle conflict

our world and at the same time draws us ever so close to God, the great paradox that can only truly make sense after one has suffered, as it would seem, through the *"lonely, dusky place."* The struggle is a result of our human experience, the lessons learned on the journey that eventually leads us back into the arms of the One who created us, bruised and battered, yet changed and secure. Conflict by its very definition is designed to clash with our personal interests and temperament when matched up in a desired relationship with the living God. By virtue of our sinful nature, we live in daily opposition with the forces of our soul and our longing for a connection with Christ. It is the great conflict that man has been fighting with since Adam. It's the human struggle with a loving God who is constantly beckoning us toward a high-water mark that we feel, more often than not, is impossible to reach. It's in the solace of knowing that *"I am with you always"* (Matthew 28:20) that becomes the only place of true hope that we can find on this road trip called life. *good reminder*

The Hope in Romans 7 and 8

Looking closely at Romans 7:14–25, we can see—and no doubt relate to—the struggle that the apostle Paul speaks of. His mind seems divided. His struggle is apparent, but his passion for victory and resolve is also obvious. He laments; *Great word!*

(vs 16) "[F]or I am not practicing what I would like to do, but I am doing the very thing I hate." (vs 18) "For I know that nothing good dwells in me, that is, in my flesh; for the willing is present in me, but the doing of the good is not. (vs 21) "I find then the principle that evil is present in me, the one who wants to do good." (vs 24) "Wretched man that I am! Who will set me free from the body of this death?" (vs 25) "Thanks be to God through Jesus Christ our Lord!"

to be holy / action of doing right

This passage of scripture grips us because we immediately understand it and can relate to what it's saying in real time through real-life experiences. It connects with us because we see ourselves being lived out in it. It would seem as though Paul is living in our skin and blurting out, as if in surround sound and 3-D images, the struggle we go through on a daily basis. When Romans 7 is read, just about everyone who longs to serve God and yet struggles gets it.

Romans 7 tells us about the Christian life as we actually experience it much of the time. Paul is not talking about the life of an unbeliever here, nor is he describing an immature or a carnal Christian. I believe Paul is trying to paint for us the typical struggle that all believers encounter in their walk with Jesus. Actually, when I read this passage, what I see is Paul's autobiography of his own personal faith walk as a broken, struggling follower of Messiah. It appears to be the apostle's actual experience of trying to walk out his day-to-day battle between holiness and humanity.

If we conclude and can admit to seeing the division and challenge that a struggling soul goes through in Romans 7, then can we also see that it becomes extremely difficult, if not impossible, to live at a level that totally prevents life's struggles from happening? It's the purpose of the enemy to make God's people feel as if they're *subnormal* believers because of their struggle, consequently never really feeling secure in Christ's love and grace. There is nothing that I can see or seems to suggest that we are to live in Romans 8 while not living in Romans 7. If we truly believe that *"Therefore there is now no condemnation for those who are in Christ Jesus"* (8:1), then Romans 7 becomes the reason and purpose for that statement—*"And I know that nothing good lives in me, that is, in my sinful nature. I want to do what is right, but I can't."* (7:18)

feelings cannot be a barometer *cautious*
feelings are deeply STRUGGLING WELL *they can*
personal to us *lie to you*

We must see that our struggle against sin and our longing to not commit sin is a division of mind that God both understands and does not condemn us in. He is keenly aware of our anguish and has provided, through His Son, great grace that becomes more than sufficient for the battle.

More times than not, we describe a hypocrite as someone who says one thing and does another. However, we may want to take an objective second look at that saying when evaluating ourselves. It fits pretty well in our theology when describing both Pharisees and Sadducees, or that two-faced friend who promised that he would keep your personal conversation private and didn't, but that definition can get a little murky when you place yourself in the equation. In other words, how do you measure yourself—by the same standard you measure others? Do you struggle with giving others grace, or do you seldom give yourself grace yet give grace to others?

Is it just me or have you noticed that followers of Jesus are not perfect? Our imperfections and shortcomings make me wonder at times if it isn't part of the job description for being a child of God. If we were advertising the prerequisites for Christianity, it might read something like this: **Wanted:** *imperfect human, one who struggles in life yet loves God intently, must be prepared to fight with guilt and condemnation, cannot give up, even when failure occurs, willing to do daily battle with principalities of darkness and one who always relies on Christ's unconditional love … even when one doesn't feel it.*

You see, what appears to be a divided mind, being viewed by someone on the outside, may actually be an internal struggle the person is going through on the inside, and that isn't necessarily a bad thing. It's possible that a divided mind can be both bad as well as good. If you've become comfortable in your sin and just don't care to move out of that sin position or address it in any way, then that, of

The anguish and pain isn't worth life.

23

course, is a bad place to be. However, if you find yourself caught in your own personal "Jabbok" (like Jacob) and are wrestling with the forces of good and evil, then this experience becomes neither ungodly nor unhealthy. If you're one of the souls that have become dazed, confused, alone, wounded, and questioning, but yet still looking for God to show up through the cannon smoke of the enemy's artillery, then you're struggling and, I would suggest, struggling well.

Spiritual life and vitality is found as much in the struggle as it is on the mountain peaks of victory. Actually, it's my experience with people that the struggle, the divided mind as it would appear, encompasses our life journey more so than the times of mental clarity, emotional stability, and spiritual bliss. Consequently we learn more from the struggle because, frankly, we spend more time there. As a result, our human and spiritual formation meet at times in a cascade of pain and healing, self-deprecation and confidence, desperation and peace, closeness to God and a sea apart from Him.

Isn't that what Paul is really trying to convey to us in Romans 7 when he says, *"I find then the principle that evil is present in me, the one who wants to do good?"* It's an acknowledgement of his human depravity, the thing that Paul had to fight with 24/7. It's the self-pleasing leftover tsunami from the Fall trying to claim us daily. It's as if the apostle is saying, *Yes, I'm a divided man, a man who struggles with sin, things that human souls struggle with. But, thanks be to God through Jesus Christ our Lord because, through it all, there is yet victory!*

You see, it's all part of the larger journey that makes up both the sweet-love relationship that we have with our Christ and King and the internal struggle that makes that relationship so difficult to maintain. It's the *creation* trying to interact with the *Creator* while at the same time trying to not feel that you don't stack up.

It's very important to see that when striving for the *"upward call of God in Christ Jesus"* (Philippians 3:14) in your faith walk, you also understand that two plus two, with God, doesn't always equal four—sometimes it equals sixteen! Things on the journey don't always line up as evenly, uniformly, clearly, or as pristine as you think they should.

Ideals are healthy things to have and to uphold. However, they are only brought to fruition as we realize that they are tested by trial and error.

Our walk with the Lord is at times like a violent storm that would appear to shake every part of our emotional, spiritual, and physical being. Elijah put it best when he said in 1 Kings 19:4, *"I have had enough, LORD…. Take my life; I am no better than my ancestors."* Yeah, even for the believer life can surely get confusing.

The Sneak Ups

Shy of building a doctrinal case—which is not the intent of this book—we as believers in Christ understand that extramarital affairs (adultery) are contrary to the teachings of Jesus, as well as being and relationally destructive.

They cannot be condoned in any form. With that being said, we have to also realize that affairs do exist in the Body of Christ and, unfortunately, are being seen in larger numbers as time goes on.

There are basically two kinds of affairs, *sexual* and *emotional*. When looking closely at the pathology behind these two types of affairs, there are often clear reasons as to why they happen. I'll be addressing in another chapter of this book the struggles of sexual addiction, and sexual affairs will be mentioned in that segment.

However, in this chapter I'd like to touch on the *emotional* affair, which can potentially prove to be, at times, the more damaging of the two. This is when an emotional attraction can gravitate into *forbidden love*. This occurs when a man and a woman who are separately married find themselves having fallen in love with each other even though they realize that they should not, cannot, and must not have anything to do with the other. Consequently, the battle that they fight between right and wrong, spiritual and human, moral and immoral erupts into a raging storm of contradiction and passion within them. They are thrown into a divided mind that clashes between conflicting worlds and is made manifest through a deep emotional connection between two unfortunate souls. These are people who should not be experiencing the feelings that they now commonly share, but nonetheless it is where they find themselves. When this happens between two Christians, sadly the emotional, marital, moral, and Biblical complications that arise from these feelings can at times be substantial and even severe.

As a therapist and minister, these cases can become some of the most heart-wrenching and emotionally complicated of all. I'm very familiar with the scriptures regarding lustful thoughts, desires of the flesh, passions, etc. and the sin attached to them. These are certainly areas that are up for Biblical discussion and should be. But again, my intent in this book is not to theologically dissect nor necessarily overly defend every opinion or example that I give. These opinions are based purely from extensive counseling sessions throughout the years with wounded and heartbroken believers. These struggling people very much want to be faithful to God's Word while at the same time find themselves in the most confusing emotional quagmire that they've ever experienced. I do believe my opinions have Biblical merit and sensibility attached to them, but the conclusion of these opinions I leave up to the reader.

There are some who might say, "Aren't they already in sin because of the *feelings* that they share for one another, knowing that they are married people?" Realizing that circumstances, passions, and intent are multidimensional, in the case I just described I would say no, in particular where there is the clear absence of sexual contact (never happened) and the deliberate and ongoing success of distancing themselves from one another. I know that statement may be shocking to some evangelicals, but allow me to explain.

The Bible clearly is not silent when it comes to the act of committing adultery. However, is temptation in and of itself a sin? If it were, then it would appear that Jesus sinned in Matthew 4:1 because it says; *"Then Jesus was led by the Spirit into the wilderness to be tempted by the devil."* A separately married man and woman who have not been intimate with each other and have successfully fought the temptation and desire to be with one another (staying apart) though they have fallen in love I would say are not in sin. Painfully unfortunate? Yes. But not sinning.

even Jesus needed H.S. to overcome Satan

I like the way the J.B. Phillips New Testament puts it regarding temptation (vs) sin in (James 1:14–15). *"No, a man's temptation is due to the pull of his own inward desires, which can be enormously attractive. His own desire takes hold of him, and that produces sin.* It's when he or she has allowed themselves to be "pull[ed] by [their] inward desires" to a place of sexual adultery that sin has then been "birth[ed]." Phillips goes on to say in verse 16, *"And sin in the long run means death."* In other words, if a person continues to live in that state of mind or any openly sinful state of mind with no regard for God's Word, then without repentance death is the outcome. The actual meaning of the word "death" is open to theological debate.

Jesus was led into the wilderness to be tempted. Well, we know that Jesus didn't sin, so there must be more than meets the eye when

27

it comes to many of life's complicated encounters. One size really doesn't fit all when it comes to life's sneak-ups. Temptation takes a progressive path toward eventual moral decline (sin). It doesn't always happen in one fell swoop! Again, I think the progression is pretty clear in James 1:14–15. First there is temptation. If that isn't effectively addressed at that stage, it will give way to lust, then sin, then death. So, temptation is a power, an influence that's designed to try and confuse us to a place where our moral equilibrium is thrown off balance. Some people are more influenced by the effect than others.

So, to repeat, where there is absence of sexual contact and clear attempt to distance themselves from one another, there is then the presence of obedience to God's Word. As to the feelings that exist between the two unfortunate lovers … that's where the grace of God comes in. Call it their "thorn in the flesh," their "cross to bear," their "burden to carry" or whatever else you may choose to name it— but after numerous acts of obedience and thousands of prayers in thousands of different ways to remove the love they share, it is God in the end who must sustain the brokenhearted. In a way, it's as if they are suspended in a painful love purgatory.

The emotional affair, when compounded by a deep, passionate love and respect that both parties share for each other, is indeed the most painful of all affairs from my professional perspective. It's what they know that shouldn't be happening to them, and often they don't want to happen to them, yet it is a place where they find themselves nonetheless. Only by spending endless hours with God in such cases and with a *determined* resolve to forge ahead for the purpose of healing can they ultimately find peace.

Our human voyage with Jesus is a mixture of excitement, discouragement, vitality, fatigue, success, failure, joy, anger, spiritual steadiness, and emotional vertigo. Hard times are inevitable. It would appear that in one day you seem to be walking steady with confidence on life's icy pond, and all of a sudden a *sneak up* appears behind you that you weren't prepared for. You're startled. Then you lose your balance. You notice you're now beginning to slip all over the ice. You reach out for something to try and stabilize yourself, but there's nothing there. As much as you try there doesn't seem to be anything that's stable to hold on to, and you begin to lose your footing quickly. Like a person dazed and disoriented you prepare for the fall...and then BAM, the next thing you know you're on the ice with a knot on your head and a bloody nose! Normally there are reasons why these circumstances happen. To become ever so keen with the needs and issues going on in your life and within your marital relationship, before the 2x4 meets your head, may end up covering "a multitude of sin" as well as avoiding a lot of emotional pain in the long term.

Temptation, Our Weird Friend

Temptation is both a hugely powerful, seductive, and enjoyable stimulant and a deceptive self-destroying landmine. It is the great contradiction that every soul struggles with, and will continue to struggle with, this side of eternity. As I just mentioned, there are times when two separately married people find themselves in the heartbreaking misfortune and untimely place in life where chemistry, morals, and God collide. They struggle with finding themselves having fallen in love outside of the covenant bond with their spouse. The temptation can seem overpowering, and the emotional struggle beyond painful and exhausting. Yet even through this they can struggle well if they are determined with their hope in Christ. You can't always evade temptation. However, you can choose to counter its gravitational pull. Walt Weber

What is temptation, and what does it look like? Let me paint it for you like the following lines.

It's very much like a man-eating lion, with a steel chain around his neck, tethered to a steel spike driven deeply into the ground. Along comes Fred when seemingly out of nowhere this 500 pound, predatory, flesh-ripping machine suddenly lunges himself at me! After the paralyzing shock and horror wears off, I realize that the lion, limited by his chain, was a good 20 feet away. So after thanking God that I still have all four limbs and a torso, I run away from the lion! Now being aware of where the lion is, I'm somewhat emotionally prepared to meet him when I travel the road again because I realize that he's tethered and can only lunge so far. Looking at his majestic beauty and strength from a distance, I'm mesmerized and begin to think to myself, *I wonder just how close I can get to this unbelievable beast and still remain safe?* So each time I walk that road and come upon the lion, out of curiously I inch closer and closer. Each time he thrusts himself at me I'm becoming more keenly aware that he can only come so far to me and no further unless I move into his sphere of death. All of a sudden I feel empowered, in control, and maybe have even a slight feeling of superiority knowing that the lion can make an intimidatingly loud noise, but, as long as I am a safe distance on the other side of that steel chain, that's all he can do. Note here that the phrase "safe distance" is a relative term and it means different things to different people. What I might think is safe you might see as unsafe. Little by little each time I walk the road I find myself getting closer and closer and closer still until suddenly, the lion has me in his clutches, and then in his mouth and finally … I'm dinner!

So the lion then becomes the warning that James was trying to communicate to us in James 1:14–15. Your coming up on a lion does not make you at fault (temptation), but to continue to fraternize with him could equal imminent destruction (sin/death).

Temptation and our struggle go hand in hand. To know your weakness is wise. To deny that you struggle is naïve. Herein lies God's grace. Sometimes you have the advantage of being aware of your weakness, and other times you don't. It can sneak up on you like a sucker punch, knocking you down dazed and confused, wobbling to get up, and finding it very difficult to do so. But it is there, just like the apostle Paul, where we each can find sweet sufficient grace in the heat of the struggle, yes, even in the great challenge of the temptation.

When a person succumbs to temptation, it weakens them and can numb them to the voice of the Holy Spirit if they don't get their spiritual sea legs balanced quickly. The enticements of the flesh are so powerful and hypnotic that they have literally ruined throughout time the best of all of us. C.S. Lewis clearly understood its allurement when he said, *"Only those who try to resist temptation know just how strong it is. We never find out the strength of the evil impulse inside us until we try to fight it."* Temptation has the power, if given into its capacity, to greatly reduce the awareness of our destructibility to a false belief in our indestructability. It is that insidious and that deceptive. King David did not take another man's wife and then have her husband killed because he was keenly aware of his tendency toward sexual addiction and homicidal thinking. No, it incubated over time while he wondered just how close he could get to the *lion* while still feeling a sense of control and restraint over its intense charm and mesmerizing power. A soul can quickly split into a divided mind once temptation is allowed to move to the dangerous place of sin. At this point, our ability to resist then becomes numbed and the pleasure center of our brain takes over and now we're talking about a dopamine free-for-all!

Clinically speaking, when a person gives into temptation, bursts of stimulating oxytocin and opiate-powered endorphins take over the limbic system part of the brain. This then connects with the prefrontal cortex, leaving it in a chemically uncontrolled feeding frenzy! Sensibility, sound judgment, and spiritual perception are basically thrown out the window while every stimulating emotional feeling in your body seems to be thrusting itself down the narrow darkened tube that leads to trouble...very possibly big trouble! If this process is not stopped, its inevitable end is then to give birth to death (separation from God).

But is *temptation* in and of its self a sin for a person to experience? If it were, then it sure would appear that Jesus sinned in Matthew 4:1 because it says, *"Then Jesus was led by the Spirit into the wilderness to be tempted by the devil."* Well, we know that Jesus didn't sin, so there must be more than meets the eye regarding temptation. As a therapist and former pastor, I see both the Biblical truth of this issue as well as the emotional and psychological trek that a person naturally goes through when battling this mind-whipping foe. Temptation takes a progressive path toward potential decline (sin). It doesn't always happen in one fell swoop! I think the progression is pretty clear in James 1:14–15. First there is temptation, and then if that isn't effectively addressed, it will give way to lust, then sin, then death. It's the being "carried away" in (vs 14) that gets us into trouble. Clearly temptation is a power that affects each and every one of us and some of us more so than others

As you can see, there are stages that follow temptation that can lead to separation from God with our sin. But being tempted by itself is not a sin.

good in temptation —humility
—reduces pride
— smugness-self-righteousness

It's the decisions that we make and the shifting of our thought patterns that we set in place that make the difference between life and death. There are times that we can handle this flurry of attacks in our lives, and other times we can't. Because the enemy knows every one of our weaknesses, he'll attempt to hit us harder in the weakest areas that we struggle in. Here's where damage control comes in handy. If you're finding that a temptation keeps orbiting around you like a gnat in your nose and you just can't keep it at bay, then professional counseling may very well be a good alternative to the "lion" that's waiting to devour you. Wanting to resolve a potentially devastating and persistent issue in your life could make the difference between struggling well and spiritual schizophrenia. *positive about temptation*

But, oddly enough, succumbing to temptation does something to a Jesus follower. It reduces their sense of being impenetrable. It erases any remnant of smugness and self-righteousness that may have once dominated their opinion of themselves. It places them in the category of soldiers who have engaged on the field of battle, were wounded, and now find themselves staring in reflective shock while they try to recover from what they've been through. To fall off one's own pedestal in the presence of others or just within his or her own private life experience gives birth to humility, which in turn encourages honesty and empathy. It was humility and honesty before God that made David say in Psalm 139:23–24; from *The Message*—

> Investigate my life, O God,
> find out everything about me;
> Cross-examine and test me,
> get a clear picture of what I'm about;
> See for yourself whether I've done anything wrong
> then guide me on the road to eternal life.

Pride = artificial
humility = real

Thomas Merton said, *"Pride makes us artificial and humility makes us real."* The cool thing about God is that even when we find ourselves in a battered and humiliated stage of life, still God lovingly reaches His hand out to pick us back up and hold us close to Him. It's almost as if we're not clearly able to see the foolishness of what we've become until we're whacked across the head and the bubble on the level is brought back to balance in our lives. This surely must be what Job meant when he said in Job 42:5, *"I have heard of You by the hearing of the ear, but now my eye sees You."* It's one thing to experience God outside of personal tragedy or failure, but something altogether different to experience Him while in it. It almost seems as if everything changes. Your mind, thinking pattern, senses, and response all seem different, almost foreign to what you have been used to experiencing in your spiritual walk. Where there was a free flow of life-giving exchange and movement between you and God, now all looks cloudy and unstable. The things that worked are now not working. The things that mattered seem now at a distance as your stained-glass Christian life is shattered in a thousand pieces and scattered in front of you. Time and space stand still. The many things that were so familiar and stable before are now shrouded within the fragile divide of the known and now unknown. There is a sense of instability, a kind of "firmly planted in air" feeling. There is a loss of the foundation that you've been building on for years that now makes you feel you are in an emotional free fall. Though there is always great grace and forgiveness for all of us who have given into temptation, still there is often that lonely and silent journey back to center that must be taken by the offender. More often than not the way back home is traveled down a path of misty fog and feeling alone, as well as around a bend of questions, tears, and self-reflection. It's there that we run head-on into ourselves, never to be the same again. Joseph Chilton Pearce said, *"Seeing within changes one's outer* vision." Often visceral and honest self-evaluation really only come to fruition as we're faced with some sort of a personal crossroad or failure in our lives. It's there that self-reflection is born … and that's a good thing.

To quote Saint Augustine, *"Humility is the foundation of all the other virtues…."* In other words, there is nothing within myself that can diminish my true sin nature and give me the "right stuff" to virtuously and morally make it in life. God-exemplified integrity doesn't naturally exist in me, so when I think *I'm all of that* … really I'm just nothing more than a flimsy, weak, counterfeit *appearance* of the real thing. Our wounded self is recessed deep within all of us. It's dormant, subdued, yet very much alive and waiting for the right moment to come out and the right environment to be placed into.

The enemy's relentless push to try and thrust his way through the believer's mind, heart, and resolve is powerful beyond our human comprehension. It is so powerful, so diabolical, and so immensely destructive that only the *grace* of God through Christ has been designed to be large enough and effective enough to counter its death sentence in the struggling soul of man. As we battle temptation, or even humiliation, there remains, as Martin Luther said, *"the great fire of the love of God for us."* Yes, a divided mind doesn't feel like an opportune place for any of us to pitch our tent. However, it is a place where we find ourselves from time to time on our human journey, not wanting but nonetheless experiencing. Yet we're beyond blessed to have, even in the form of a whispered prayer, the great neutralizer to our convoluted minds and struggling souls. The answer? Christ's great and extravagant grace as well as His selfless and endlessly unconditional *agape* love, above all things the most powerful redemptive force unprecedented and matchless under all circumstances!

2

OUR HUMAN CONDITION

"Mysterious though it is, the characteristics in human nature which we love best grow in a soil with a strong mixture of troubles."

~ Harry Emerson Fosdick

Let's break this human idea down. According to the "Humanist Doctrine of Man," the humanist believes that man is a part of nature, and that he has emerged as the result of a continuous process. The humanistic philosophy is atheistic in nature and materialistic in application. When someone denies the reality of God, they remove that which makes a man … a man. In Biblical reality, there can be no "manhood" without "Godhood." Nonetheless, with the humanist, man stands alone without the existence of a Divine Creator.

Since humanists begin with man, they attribute to him the exalted position of the highest being. God is dethroned and man is deified. Basically, humanism is the worship of man. As the highest being, his thoughts and actions are always right. There should be no feelings of guilt, shame, regret or a sense of moral right and wrong because in the eyes of the humanist, these feelings are nonexistent.

To them, there is no God, so there is no afterlife. As a result, there are no consequences to sin because sin doesn't exist.

On the other hand, there's the Bible that says man is a creation of God: *"So God created human beings in his own image. In the image of God he created them; male and female he created them."* (Gen. 1:27) God hardwired man to possess mental faculties by which he can know and understand the things of God, and the intelligence to choose between right and wrong. This of course speaks to man's moral responsibility. The Bible says that man has a purpose for living. This purpose is for him to glorify God in all that man does (1 Cor. 10:32). Not only does man have a purpose on earth, but this purpose far transcends this planet that we live on. The nature of man necessitates an eternal purpose. Therefore, God has lovingly set eternity in man's heart as a natural homing device. (Ecclesiastes 3:11)

While man enjoys freedom and liberty, he doesn't make license out of this liberty. There are restrictions on freedom, limitations on liberty (Gal. 5:13). Freedom is enjoyed as we live within the confines of God's Word because it provides protection and a moral balance to our otherwise selfish lives. Man doesn't have the freedom to do as he pleases. Freedom is not a question of doing what we like but rather doing what is right and selfless.

Humanists are about forgetting God and serving themselves, and Christianity is about acknowledging God and serving Him rather than themselves. What happens to man and God when man screws up? Does God take into account our human condition when we sin? Or does He expect us to always transcend above our human, sinful, collapsed state when we fall short of His Word and we make a mistake?

I really think we need to see something here, because if not, then the bar in our relationship with God will be so high that none of us

will ever be able to reach it. *We put great expectation on our faith, while allowing little to no tolerance for our humanity.* We need to wrap our minds around the fact that we are both. We're both intense lovers of Christ and the truth of His Word as well as genetic recipients of the greatest, catastrophic, human meltdown in history … the Fall of Man. Acknowledging our human condition isn't going light on our sin. It's having confidence in His great agape that when we do sin, we're not disqualified. Martin Luther said, *"Faith is a living, daring confidence in God's grace, so sure and certain that a man could stake his life on it a thousand times."* This coming from a man who deeply loved Jesus, pioneered the Reformation, and drank way more beer than he should have. Oh, my evangelical!

Where's the Empathy?

Here's one of a number of true stories. A pastor and his wife came to me for counseling from out of state. A staff member walked into the pastor's study and surprisingly caught him viewing pornography. The staff member told an elder in the church what he had witnessed. That understandably led to the elders meeting with the pastor and discussing this concerning issue. The leadership decided to place the pastor on a three-month sabbatical with the understanding that he seek counseling for his problem. The pastor and his wife counseled with me in an Intensive Out Patient (IOP) setting for three days (16 hours). That's a lot of time to find out about someone's life. When dealing with sin issues, we so often look at just the *symptom* (the in-your-face sin) rather than the *cause* (the pathology) of why the sin happened in the first place. Isn't that what God did in Genesis the 4th chapter?

jealousy

Symptom: Cain kills his brother Abel. **Cause:** Cain had anger toward God because he felt God always chose his brother over him. God was concerned for Cain and even asked him, *"Why are you angry?"* Unfortunately for Cain, he didn't go there with God. The answers are always in the why, not the actual act of sin. That's hard for us evangelicals to understand because we're trained to punish sin first, then when there's change, we'll embrace you back in the fold...but often at a distance. This is what happened to the pastor who was caught viewing pornography. We went into many of the causes regarding this issue, and by the grace of God made real progress. The problem was when he went back home, he was fired! The leaders felt that there had to be a statement made for "purity's sake" within the church. That meant that the pastor had to leave and a new one was going to be brought in. I couldn't help asking one of the elders if he had ever viewed porn. He said that question was irrelevant. I then said, "This man trusted you with his position as well as his family, and in return you gave him the left foot of fellowship!" I then asked how many leaders were on the church board. He gave me a number. I closed by saying that there was a very good likelihood that at least two or three of these leaders are viewing pornography as well. You see, they reacted to the pastor's sin while not taking more of an interest in helping him through the *cause* of that sin. It's difficult to be empathetic with others when our pharisaical religious upbringing blinds us from the truth of ... *"You who are without sin cast the first stone"* (John 8:7). Jesus understood and is showing us in this verse that it was a result of this women's *human condition* that brought her to the point of selling herself into prostitution. Whether that sin is falling so low that you're selling yourself for someone else's sexual pleasures or you're a Christian and find yourself trapped in viewing pornography or struggling with an out-of-control anger issue, in the end our human condition is all the same in all sin categories. God doesn't measure sin on some spiritual Richter scale. One sin doesn't outweigh another in God's eyes. In (Romans 6:23) it says that *"the wages of sin is death."* That means if you're dishonest on your income taxes, gorge yourself with food or commit an act of adultery, when it comes to God viewing sin, it's all the same.

There are evangelicals, if not overtly certainly covertly, who see certain sins as different from one another with different penalties attached to them. One example is homosexuality. The evangelical stance on same-sex attraction is famous to say the least. To most evangelicals, homosexuality is a sin that is much more terrible and despicable than, say, lying or gossip. In Biblical reality, these are all sins that separate us from God and therefore worthy of repentance. Yet, lying and gossip, though not condoned in the evangelical community, are more spiritually and socially palatable than the sin of homosexuality. One is distained much more than the others. Why? Because there's been this pervasive mentality instilled within evangelicals for multiple decades that says you can somehow merge Old Testament *Law* with New Testament *Grace*. Therefore, grace seems to be extended more freely to the one who has lied or gossiped than the person who is struggling with same-sex attraction. Judgment is pronounced more severely on the homosexual because it's a more "detestable act" (Leviticus. 18:22 NET)—yet again forgetting Jesus' New Testament words: *"You who are without sin cast the first stone"* (John 8:7). Sin was sin with Jesus…no more of this one sin being worse than the other.

However, there is a sin that many of us carry around often throughout our lives that is, like all other sins, detestable to God as well. I'm talking about the sin of *unforgiveness*. Jesus tells us in Mark 6:15, *"But if you refuse to forgive others, your Father will not forgive your* sins." Wow... that's a mind blower! So, how do we skirt around this statement from Jesus as we're weighing the different sins of those we come in contact with? The evangelical mindset, though realizing that unforgiveness is Biblically wrong, seems more willing to extend grace to the unforgiving saint than to the person struggling with homosexuality. Though you may feel this is a "detestable" sin for the person struggling with same-sex attraction, yet can you extend that same grace to this person as you would someone who has an issue forgiving people? And if not, then isn't that hypocritical? I think that Jesus may have had situations like this in mind when He said in (Matthew 7:4–5); *"How can you say to your brother, 'Let me take the speck out of your eye,' when all the time there is a plank in your own eye?* ⁵ *You hypocrite, first take the plank out of your own eye, and then you will see clearly to remove the speck from your brother's eye."* If we're not applying New Testament, Jesus grace on ALL sins, then in actuality aren't we really just trying to amalgamate Old Testament law into New Testament grace and, in the end, stand as a judge as to which one is worse than the other? Well, guess what? Jesus made it so it doesn't work that way anymore. Thank God!

No more having to "stack up" to the Law in order to receive God's forgiveness or favor. To place the Law first in our lives greatly minimizes God's grace that's found in our Messiah as well as the great sacrifice that He paid to provide that grace. For the blinded, pious crimes of empty virtue are for others to commit. Oh, to God that we rip all pharisaical mentality from our hearts!

It Was a Hard Fall

C.S. Lewis said, *"Aim at heaven and you will get earth thrown in. Aim at earth and you get neither."* If we're to be completely honest with God in His call for us to "walk in Him" (Col.2:6), then we also have to be honest about the condition of the feet of clay that's making that walk.

We need to understand crystal clearly the immense human catastrophic blunder that happened in the moments of Genesis 3:7 when it says, *"Then the eyes of both of them were opened, and they knew that they were naked...."* In man's short *sinless* existence with Father God (Gen. 1:27–3:7), the sweet relationship that they briefly shared together went from tranquil, secure and close to unstable, troubled, and distant.

Yes, man had fallen. Everything about man changed in those few moments of disobedience. Psychologically, emotionally, physically, neurologically, biologically, and spiritually Adam and Eve would never be the same again. And if that weren't bad enough, they would pass that total human disturbance (fallen condition) on to every generation of human beings that followed them.

It was an absolute disastrous human mess! For example, our bodies became damaged and weakened, now susceptible to diseases. The immune system, a network of cells, tissues, and organs that work together to defend the body against attacks by "foreign" invaders, was compromised. The body was now open to killer microbes, organisms, bacteria, and viruses that could take it out (potentially with great pain) in a moment's time.

The limbic system of the brain, the part that expresses emotion, behavior, motivation, memory, mood, pleasure, fear, anger, sex drive, rationality, and attention is now all twisted. As a result, it can misfire and REACT uncontrollably, irrationally, and irresponsibly at any time depending on the issue or environment that it finds itself in. And as for the spiritual condition of man...it's now all been literally "shot to hell!"

As you can see, if we don't factor in the enormity of all of these human destructive complications regarding the fall of man, then we're being dishonest about the truth of our fallen nature as well as looking at our faith walk only one-dimensionally. And if we're dishonest about that, then how will we ever be able to truly appreciate and love the great tolerant grace of God that He's freely given us in Christ? It's because of our inherited "fallenness" and propensity to screw up that God has made available His lavished agape (love) to all mankind through the sacrifice of His Son, Jesus. That means Christ's agape and death on the cross was specifically accomplished, purposed, and molded around man's fallen nature. To "walk in Him" is a life journey, a marathon not a sprint that requires submitting this human condition into the loving and grace-filled hands of our Abba, Father. It's He alone who is fully able to understand the true meaning of the word *restoration* (to repair something to its original condition). Restoring us back to Him has been completely and thoroughly provided for through Christ's death, burial, and resurrection. Each one of us has a specific purpose in God's larger plan. We must comprehend that the beautiful power of agape and grace has been given by God through His Son, Jesus, to rescue fallen man from the penalty of death (Adam's disobedience). Eternity is not based on what we can *do* to make ourselves more righteous and worthy to get there, but rather it's solely founded on what God has done *for us in Christ* that *makes us* worthy and righteous enough to spend eternity with Him. In and of ourselves we possess nothing that helps heal our damaged human state. We are all desperately in need of an advocate Redeemer. The plain truth is we are deeply, radically, and unconditionally loved by Jesus Christ. And it's this love that drove Him to the cross to pay for our sins, and we have done nothing to earn it or deserve it. It was *love* that paid the ransom for our redemption, and anything else contrary to this reality is a religious counterfeit.

Jesus understands the conflicting behavior that believers struggle with when it comes to serving Him daily. Brennan Manning put it best when he said , *"When I get honest, I admit I am a bundle of paradoxes. I believe and I doubt, I hope and get discouraged, I love and I hate, I feel bad about feeling good, I feel guilty about not feeling guilty. I am trusting and suspicious. I am honest and I still play games."* These are the things that God knows about His kids because He understands just how far they've fallen.

God Gets Our Suffering

The Christian philosopher Alvin Plantinga said, "[God] enters into and shares our suffering. He endures the anguish of seeing His son, the second person of the Trinity, consigned to the bitterly cruel and shameful death of the cross. Some theologians claim that God cannot suffer. I believe they are wrong. God's capacity for suffering, I believe, is proportional to His greatness; it exceeds our capacity for suffering in the same measure as His capacity for knowledge exceeds ours."

According to Plantinga, God has, through His son, addressed the areas that have plagued mankind since Adam fell, that being sin, suffering, and death. And in doing this, God also addressed our broken down and tattered relationship with Him and how it has been repaired for us in Christ. The writer of Hebrews tells us in 4:15,

"For we do not have a high priest who is unable to empathize with our weaknesses, but we have one who has been tempted in every way, just as we are—yet he did not sin." What a friend we have

If this is true, then Christ not only went through pain and sorrow for us, but He also feels our pain and sorrow in our real-time life experiences. This also includes His connecting with us through the

in Jesus"

45

flurry of temptation that we're hit with on a daily basis, *"tempted in every way just as we are...."* God's answer to our brokenness and human frailty is the finished work of Jesus. Only as we draw from the grace shown to us through His sacrifice can we truly understand and settle once and for all that death, condemnation, guilt, and shame was nailed to the cross for our relational emancipation with God.

We have to remember that faith in Christ Jesus is not an immunizing medication against pain, sorrow, temptation, or even failure in our lives, but it is the only source of authentic stability one can possess that is psychologically and emotionally designed to effectively combat the enemy's reign of death on us. C.S. Lewis in his book, *The Problem of Pain*, said, *"Try to exclude the possibility of suffering which the order of nature and the existence of freewill involve, and you find that you have excluded life itself."* Suffering is real because we are real. Our human condition dictates that life will not be a bed of roses for us. As much as we don't want to think of it, life often hurts and none of us want to hurt. Adam did us no favor with his act of self-pleasing and self-centeredness in the garden. All hell (literally) broke loose on man that day, and there's nothing that we can do about that. Like it or not, we are all descendants of Adam and therefore have inherited his curse of death. However, our benevolent and loving God through His Son, Jesus, has seen our desperate state and hasn't left us abandoned in hopelessness. We need to know that His Word is true and His promises forever faithful in all aspects of our fallen nature.

Adam Young summed it up this way: *"I am fallen, flawed, and imperfect. Yet drenched in the grace and mercy that is found in Jesus Christ."* Now, if that doesn't leave you feeling hopeful as you get muddied up in this life, then I don't know anything that will.

all the Satan wants to throwback to our faces is

accuser of brethein

HowCan a good God be capable of cursing Man?

3

THE HOLY AND BROKEN

"Accepting the reality of our broken, flawed lives is the beginning of spirituality not because the spiritual life will remove our flaws but because we let go of seeking perfection and, instead, seek God, the one who is present in the tangled-ness of our lives."

— Michael Yaconelli

There has been a lot of emphasis placed within the evangelical church in the last forty-plus years on the *victory* and *success* side of our Christian life. Yes, there certainly is some validity with incorporating these two words within our faith walk; however, that truth becomes only one-dimensional when looking at the whole of our lives. The reality is not all of our life is victorious or successful. As a matter of fact, most of life isn't that way at all. The apostle James confirms as much when he says in (1:2–4);

"Consider it a sheer gift, friends, when tests and challenges come at you from all sides. You know that under pressure, your faith-life is forced into the open and shows its true colors. So don't try to get out of anything

prematurely. Let it do its work so you become mature and well-developed, not deficient in any way." (The Message)

Certainly God doesn't want us to live a defeated life, but the fact is people tend to become discouraged at times as they walk this challenging, pressuring, testing journey called life. And when we run head-on into these experiences, how are we supposed to deal with the reality of our feelings, thoughts, and questions? Are we to deny that they exist? What happens when it seems you've exhausted all of the faith that you have and the thing is still at large and in charge of your life? How do you handle it when you feel that God has abandoned you and the only thing that seems real at the moment is the presence of tears running down your cheeks? James was addressing the church here…Jesus' followers, yet they were people who came face-to-face with painful experiences while walking on the "Way." To put an "It's all good" tag on our human pilgrimage is neither Biblical nor honest. The truth is God is with us and even sustains us through the battering waves of life's violent storms. He's with us in the high times as well as the low times, the encouraging times as well as the sad times, the clear times as well as the questioning times of our lives. To be honest, God is there for us in ALL of life's ebbs and flows and never does He think any more or less of His children in either state. If you chart out in the ocean and stay there long enough, you'll inevitably run into a storm or it will run into you. So yes, of course He's there, but that doesn't mean that life still can't hurt.

Jesus' Knockout Punch

Try to image with me, if you would, the following revamped version of John 8:1–11—of the woman who was caught in adultery.

At about dawn, Jesus was teaching the Good News to people who were gathered around him at the temple courts. All of a sudden some teachers of the law and Pharisees abruptly paraded in front of Jesus a woman who had just been` caught in adultery and made her stand right in front of Him and all of the other people who were there. Humiliated, disgraced, and very frightened, the woman hung her head in shame and tried her best to hide her face so as not to be recognized. The self-righteous religious zealots said with a loud and pious voice, "In the Law of Moses, it says that we're to stone to death such a woman as this. What do you say, Jesus?"

Now they had him right where they wanted him! In no way is Jesus, a Jew, going to disavow the Torah and the Pentateuch, the first five books of Moses. For the "Law guys" this was the moment that they had been waiting for. The stars, sun, moon, and planets had all gathered in a glorious lineup to finally put this self-proclaimed Messiah out of business for good! It was the picture-perfect setting with the perfect question. If Jesus said, "No, you shouldn't stone her," then He would be contradicting the Law of Moses. Therefore He would be branded as a blasphemous Jewish heretic and thus a false prophet. And if He said, "Yes, you're right. She broke the Law of Moses so go ahead and stone her," then His followers would see Him as a hypocrite preaching out of both sides of His mouth, no better than the legalistic teachers of the law and Pharisees and therefore not Messiah material. He was caught in their villains' handcrafted web, personalized in the most religiously effective way to take Jesus down, bring him to trial, and finally once and for all silence His message! At least it would seem to appear that way.

But Jesus, being full of the Holy Spirit and armed with a new revolutionary and life-giving covenant from God, neither confirmed nor denied their Law-laced question meant to trap him. Instead, he just bent down and started to write something on the ground with his finger. *What's this nonsense?* the hypocritical religious leaders must have been thinking. Enraged, they hammered him all the more with questions regarding this woman and what Moses had to say about her sin.

Finally Jesus stood up, straightened himself, looked them right in the face, and let loose with one of the most self-reflective and radically powerful New Covenant statements ever made: *"Let any one of you who is without sin be the first one to throw a stone at her."* Then, as if on heavenly cue, He stooped back down and began to write something on the ground again. I wonder if Jesus was writing on the ground something new, something life-giving and redemptive as the Law guys continued to press him. Maybe Jesus was thinking of when His Father originally wrote (with His own finger) the Ten Commandments and handed them to Moses on Mount Sinai, the Law, the decree that was only designed to "hold down the fort" until the Messiah came with grace, redemption, and agape to forgive humanity when they fell short of His standards.

Jesus knew that the Old Covenant laws had been set in place *until* He (Messiah) came to fulfill them. He knew that He wasn't there for the purpose of destroying those laws, but rather to fulfill their meaning... to make them better through His sacrifice on the cross as a result of His deep love for humanity. And because He was fulfilling their meaning, it was now *unnecessary* for Jews, gentiles, or any other race to have to keep those laws of sacrifice and rituals anymore in order to be accepted by God. The promised Messiah had come! He was the "last Adam" who was from heaven and was sinless, unlike the first Adam.

The Law guys who were pressing him with the words of Moses had no idea that it was now pointless to pronounce judgment on

legalism = cheated of grace / more acceptance — victor

this woman for her sin. The Son of God was present before their very eyes, and they were all too self-righteously blind to notice Him. They cringed and were enraged at His Messianic proclamations. They were both spellbound and dripping with hatred at Jesus' wise and self-examining words. What a dramatic moment, the legalists *[Pharisees]* and the One *[Jesus]* who had now come to delegalize the very act of death these men were making on this woman. In real-time, living color, He stood before them, the fulfiller of the prophesied words in Isaiah 61; "[bringing] good news to the afflicted; [He has] sent me to bind up the brokenhearted, proclaim liberty to captives And proclaim freedom to prisoners." He was slapping their legalistic hands while at the same time coming to the rescue of a woman, and in essence all of us, who are in deep need of redemption and agape. Jesus may have been thinking when writing on the ground … *My Father wrote the Law on stone with His finger and gave it to Moses knowing that man would not be able to fulfill it without a Redeemer. I now write a new law with my finger in the dirt, the place where man began …. Let any of you who are without sin be the first to throw a stone at her."* KO'ed by a Messianic punch to their religious hypocritical jaw … from younger to older, they slowly dropped their rocks, turned, and walked away in frustrated defeat.

Jesus then said to the woman, "Where are your accusers?" She responds, "They're all gone!" He then says, "I don't accuse you either. Go home and don't return to this lifestyle anymore. It's sin, and sin will destroy you and corrupt your relationship with the Father."

If we as believers in Jesus don't see that we are all broken, leaking pots in need of repair, then we'll have a natural self-righteous tendency to be unable to see our own reflection in the mirror of human corruption. Despite what some evangelicals may say, living out life as we know it is not always a celebration of hearts and flowers. Sometimes life gets cloudy. Sometimes it rains and even other times

Satan = accuser / Jesus = no condemnation

it pours down so much that the only hope you have, metaphorically, is that God promised He wouldn't bring another flood on the earth!

Rashida Rowe said, *"We are not perfect, we have flaws, we have regrets and we make mistakes, these characteristics do not make us worthless, they make us worthy and susceptible to human error."* If we don't see ourselves as those who long to be holy as well as those who find themselves broken, then we've disregarded our fallen human propensity to naturally gravitate toward sin. Jesus spent His entire ministry around people who were both religious and deeply flawed. If we don't allow ourselves a more compassionate understanding of this, then our Christian experience could look more like self-condemnation and confusion than confidence and clarity.

Symptom/Cause

A couple came to me for counseling regarding difficulty in being able to effectively communicate with each other. Let's call them Jack and Jen. Jack was a good man and loved his wife very much, but Jack couldn't get Jen to talk about issues within the marriage or family without her emotionally retreating, getting angry, or blowing up. She really didn't want to be around a lot of people at all, and this presented a problem for Jack because he was a total "people person." After counseling with their pastor for a while, they eventually felt that they needed a more clinical/Biblical perspective on their issue, so they came to me. Their pastor felt that the matter was now in their hands and God's, and they would just have to *press in* and work through it. After talking with Jack and Jen, I got the clear impression that their pastor really didn't place a lot of stock in psychotherapy or "psychobabble" as he put it. So this was our starting point.

After a few sessions with Jack and Jen and after evaluating all of the information that they provided me, it became obvious just why Jen struggled so much with communication and anger. Jen suffered from a moderate mood disorder that left her feeling depressed, anxious, and agitated most of the time. I also found out that from ages nine through twelve years old, Jen had been sexually molested by two male family members. This was the first time that Jen had divulged this information. Jen said that she had considered sharing this information with her pastor, but because of his more legalistic slant on scripture, she didn't feel safe.

After spending some time with Jen and Jack in therapy, there began to be a clear breakthrough. Jen eventually walked to a place of forgiving her abusers of the sin and trauma that they imposed on her. She also had to walk out of the "messages and signals" that had plagued her from her childhood and were falsely defining who she was. Jen began to see and connect with the person that she *is* in Christ rather than the person she had been made to feel that she *was* as a result of her trauma. With symptoms of greatly reduced depression/anxiety as well as better communication skills, Jen is now, by the grace of God, living a quality of life with her family that she had never experienced before. Why? She decided to deal with the "cause" of her pain rather than the "symptom." As a result of the Fall, our human condition and psyche are designed in such a way that the emotional pain that we display outwardly is nothing more than a symptom of the true epicenter of pain that's going on inwardly.

Jesus and Symptom/Cause

We see a really vivid picture of this in John 4 where Jesus is holding a conversation with a Samaritan woman at the well. The woman

[handwritten: she did not seek Him / Christ sought her]

[handwritten title: Jesus sought out the the Woman at the Well]

comes to Jacob's well to draw some water to take back with her and then...BOOM...there's Jesus! He said to her—I'm taking some paraphrasing liberty here...

"Excuse me, lady, will you give me some water, please?"

The woman says, "Yeah, but you're a Jew and you're not supposed to be even talking to me because your people think we're *less than*. So how come you're asking me for a drink of water?"

Jesus said, "I understand, but if you knew the gift of God and who it is that's asking you right now for a drink, you'd be asking for some living water." *[handwritten: legalism = stinking water]*

The woman said, "Sir, you don't have anything to draw water with and this well is deep! And by the way, where can a person get this *living water* you're talking about?"

Jesus said, "You and everybody else can keep drinking the water from this well all you want, but you'll just keep getting thirsty. But I have some water that if you drink it, you'll never be thirsty again. This stuff that I have will spring up in you and become eternal life!"

The woman says, "I'm in! This is awesome! Give me this water because I don't want to thirst anymore or have to keep coming back to this well!"

Now Jesus is getting ready to zero in on the CAUSE here. He says, "Okay, but first go get your husband and then come back and see me."

She said, "I don't have a husband."

Jesus then said, "You're right. The fact is you've had five husbands plus the guy you're presently living with."

So let's take a look at this. SYMPTOM—the woman had five husbands and was now living with a man. You would think, *That's your problem, lady, you've had five husbands, that's a lot! Now, ditch this guy you're living with, get your head and heart right, and God will start blessing your life.*

But she was spiritually blind and Jesus knew this, thus the reason for Him having this conversation with her. The woman wanted to quickly change the subject because things were obviously getting uncomfortable for her. So she starts having a theological debate with Jesus about where his people and her people worship. Now, that in and of itself is funny. Can you imagine trying to hold a theological debate with the Ancient of Days, the Author and Perfecter of our faith, the Messiah King? That's like trying to throw a wrestling move on Hulk Hogan and expect him to not slam you into next Wednesday! The fact that this woman had all of these men in and out of her life actually wasn't the main problem, and Jesus knew it.

Yes, clearly it was a problem and a big one. However, when Jesus said to her, "Go call your husband," what He was actually doing was reaching into her past, her pain, and very possibly her abuse. This was the *epicenter* of her problem. What Jesus did by making that statement to her was to touch the CAUSE and reason why this woman lived such a dysfunctional and apparently sad life. He wanted so much to give her the "living water" that He was offering, but He knew that she couldn't have what He was offering and at the same time continue to live in her sin. There was a divine transformation that Jesus was offering her, but she had to get what he was saying or it would be just another religious conversation for her. After the your-people-worship-here and my-people-worship-there conversation by the woman, Jesus puts on the full court Messiah press by saying, in verse 23 and 24, "...[A] time is coming and has now come when the true worshipers will worship the Father in the Spirit and in truth, for they are the kind of worshipers the Father seeks. God is spirit, and his worshipers must worship in the Spirit and in truth." Wow! For sure this woman had never heard this kind of talk before. True worshipers? "Worshiping in Spirit and in truth?" "The Father is looking for these kind of people

Burned out on "religion"

to worship Him?" I mean, this had to have been a lot for her to take in.

She responds by saying, "I know that a Messiah (called Christ) is coming. When He comes, He'll explain everything to us."

As if the "worship in spirit and truth" statement wasn't enough, Jesus then declares to her, "Me, the one you're speaking to, I'm Him."

Jesus realized that unless the woman wanted to touch the CAUSE of why she was having so many men shooting in and out of her life, then all she would be left with would be empty dreams and a battered and abused heart...not to mention the absence of eternal life. As a result of their conversation, the woman returned to her town and said to her people, *"Come, see a man who told me everything I ever did!"* (That would be her five husbands and the guy she's now living with).

Now remember this was the "living water" He was talking to her about. She must have thought, *This is crazy to somehow think that God would allow me to be this intimate with Him knowing the kind of person that I am.*

But this is the message that God's Son was to bring, *"Are you tired? Worn out? Burned out on religion? Come to me. Get away with me and you'll recover your life. I'll show you how to take a real rest. Walk with me and work with me—watch how I do it. Learn the unforced rhythms of grace."* (Matt. 11:28–29, *The Message*). This was, in essence, what the Samaritan woman and the many people in her town heard, and as a result they became believers in Jesus and His message of the Father's love for them. Through one woman's broken, tattered, and hollow religious life, Jesus, through agape, grace, and kindness, won a whole town over to His Father. Oh, what a day! What a smile that must have put on God's face!

Jesus Rocks Peter's World

It's in John 21 where Peter went out fishing one night with a few of his disciple buddies. I wonder what he was thinking out there, what he talked about with the other Jesus guys. They must have had time for conversation because as the hours ticked by, they were catching nothing. No fish must have meant more time for talking to each other. Or did it? Actually, I wonder if there was much conversation at all between them. I can almost hear Peter halfheartedly responding to an occasional comment or story by one of the other men as his mind drifted in and out with thoughts of "that night" ... that infamous and horrible night. The human mind is made in such a way that when shocked or traumatized, your prefrontal cortex (responsible for regulating emotions and fear response) doesn't regulate or function properly. This can make a person feel reflective and frightened at any given time, in particular where there is something familiar around them that reminds the person of the trauma. Enter in perhaps a few of the disciples who are in the boat with Peter and may have been with him the night he denied Jesus.

Clinically, Peter *may* have been experiencing PTSD (Post Traumatic Stress Disorder) this fishing night ... maybe one of several times since Jesus' crucifixion. Because of the very nature of PTSD, Peter is not in a condition now to control his thoughts. His thinking patterns give way to imagery which is etched in his memory forever as a result of the night that he disavowed any knowledge at all of being with Jesus or having anything to do with Him. Slipping in and out of emotion-filled memories, with his friend's voices now muffled and faint in the background, it happens again. Peter, as if it were just yesterday rather than over a month ago, recalls standing by an open fire warming himself just outside of the high priest's courtyard.

Suddenly, a woman blurts out; "You aren't one of this man's disciples too, are you?" Peter says, "No, I'm not!" He looks around wondering if anyone else has noticed him. Then, out of nowhere, it happens a second time, "You aren't one of his disciples too, are you?" "I am not!" Again, like rapid procession, one of the high priest's servants, a relative of the man whose ear Peter cut off, said to him, "Didn't I see you with Him in the garden?" And once again Peter adamantly denied it. As the sun was just beginning to come up, he heard a rooster crow. Peter through glazed eyes and heightened anxiety then remembered what Jesus said to him, "...*Before the rooster crows today, you will deny three times that you know me.*" It's that earth-shattering and haunting crow sound perpetually ringing out in Peter's ears that won't leave him alone, the ever plaguing constant reminder of his failure and cowardice. *Why didn't I stand up and boldly proclaim that I was a follower of Messiah? Why couldn't I do it...why didn't I do it?* As Peter stares at the empty fishnet, he reflects on how this event has been played out over and over in his head for almost forty days now. It's as if someone keeps pressing the rewind button in his brain. Shock after traumatizing shock Peter keeps reliving that evening and early morning, and each time he does, he weeps bitterly and falls into deep depression. He must have thought, *Oh, God, how can I get this nightmare to stop? I'm so sorry! I hate who I am. I've sinned against Your Son. How can I possibly be forgiven for what I've done?*

The sun was just coming up and Peter and the other disciples weren't that far offshore. Just then a voice from the shoreline yelled out to them, "Friends, don't you have any fish?" Curious as to who it was, they responded, "No, nothing." The man on the shore then said, "Listen, why don't you cast your net on the right side of the boat? If you do, you'll find some fish there." Peter and the guys had been fishing all night. They were all over that body of water trying to catch some fish, but nothing, absolutely nothing all night. Now, what's all of this nonsense about throwing the net to the right side of the boat because there's fish there? Peter must have thought, *If there were fish there, wouldn't we have found them by now? Aw, what the heck, why not, what do we have to lose? We're about to come in anyway. Let's humor the guy.* So Peter cast the net where the man had directed. After just waiting a couple minutes, YAHOO ... FISH!! And not just fish, but a whole boatload of them! Peter was amazed and couldn't believe his eyes at all of the fish that were caught in his net. "Are you kidding? I mean what ... how did ... where did ... why did ... that's crazy!"

But as Peter was baffled as to the fish, John was gazing hard at the shoreline, staring, squinting his eyes, trying to make out just who this guy was who said this "right side of the boat" thing. *Wow, this feels so familiar*, John must have thought. *No way! It couldn't possibly be ... could it?* And then, in just a few seconds, he had Him clear in his sight. John stopped with the fish and turned around..."Hey, guys ... it's the Lord!"

Hearing John say, "It's the Lord!" Peter spun his head around with bulged eyes and a mesmerized stare. The amygdala part of Peter's brain shatters with emotional responses like someone shooting out a windowpane with a shotgun! With 10,000 thoughts rushing through his mind in just a matter of seconds, Peter freezes for a minute, then quickly wraps something around him and jumps into the water. He's kind of like a deer that's just been shot with an arrow and darts away in shock not knowing quite what's happened to him.

Now, you have to be open to think outside of the box here. If not, then the only conclusion one can come up with is that Peter was so excited to hear that it was Jesus on the shore that he jumped in the water and hurried with excitement to get to Him. That, of course, could very well be so. However, I'm not convinced. I personally feel that Peter was in shock (a form of trauma). Think about it. You walk closely with a man you believe to be the Messiah for three years, follow him through miracle after miracle, controversy after controversy, and have explicit and total trust in Him as the Son of God. Then in one night, with cursing on your lips, you completely disavow knowing or having anything to do with him, a full-blown denial and betrayal of everything you've believed Him to say or to be … all of this in just a matter of minutes.

Now think for a moment. If you've acted this way toward a friend and the friend knows it, just how excited would you be to talk with him again if you happened to see him at a distance? [a] Yes, I couldn't wait to see him and catch up on old times, or [b] No way! If I see him in aisle number 2 in the grocery store, I want to be in aisle number 12 hiding between moms, kids, and carts!

This is all theoretical, of course, but just try to put yourself there. Peter has now swum to shore. He stumbles as he gets out of the water, pulls himself up, and approaches Jesus in a clumsy kind of way. He looks at him, looks away, then finally makes eye contact again. "Jesus! Yeah, well, I can't believe it's you … I mean I should believe it because You said You would rise from the dead. But how'd You do that? Oh, sorry, you're the Messiah. That's easy for you, right? I heard that You've been around for some days, but I really didn't know if You were, um, I mean I should know because of all of the miracles You've performed. Oh, yeah, speaking of miracles, how are You doing with that … miracles I mean? Have you performed any lately? Sorry—wow, I mean being raised from the dead was a big miracle by itself, wasn't it? [Mumbling under his breath] "That was a stupid thing for me to say. Why'd I say that?"

Jesus, with compassionate eyes and a smile on His face, just looked at Peter as he was stumbling all over himself. Peter kept going on while Jesus stirred the hot coals of the fire that had fish cooking on it. Peter and the other disciples really hadn't eaten anything substantial since the evening before, and the aroma of the fish simmering on the fire was both a welcome blessing for Peter as well as a distraction to all that was going on around him. Just then, Thomas, Nathanael, James and John (who were also called the sons of Zebedee) and two other disciples came ashore with the net attached to the boat filled with fish. Peter, still jittery from trying to hold an awkward one-way conversation with Jesus, excused himself and ran to the boat to help the other guys bring the fish to shore.

Can you imagine what the conversation must have been like between all of those disciples as they were on the shoreline securing the fish just several feet from Jesus?

In just a few minutes and with a low tone, first—

Thomas: "Yeah, I gotta admit I doubted Him at first, but hey, that's just the way I think. Excuse me for being cerebral! Now all of you know as soon as He showed me His nail-scarred hands … I was a believer, right there on the spot. You don't think He would be upset with me over all of that doubting … would He?"

Nathanael: "Okay—yeah, it's true, I was a little skeptical about Him being the Messiah at first, you know, coming from Nazareth and all. But in the end, and all of you know this, I believed what Philip said about Him. I mean come on. You've got to remember what He said about me, right? 'Here's a man in whom there's no deception.' That's not a bad thing, right? Yeah, well I think I'm okay with Him. What do you guys think?"

[No response].

James: "Well, I remember when He called me and my brother down when we were going through that Samaritan village. You guys remember, don't you? The people didn't welcome us at all. Actually, if you recall, they were downright angry with us. What would you do? That just really ticked us off, so yeah, we asked Jesus if He wanted us to call down fire from heaven and destroy all of them. I mean … we were really only half serious, but He did rebuke us for it."

John: Yeah … well, I'm not so much worried about that as much as the rough position Mom put us in with Him. I mean … that was really uncomfortable when she asked Him if He would put me and James on His right side and His left when He comes into His Kingdom. I mean, she even said, "Jesus, will You do me a favor … a FAVOR!' Like somehow He's a connected heavenly politician who can hook you up and pull some strings with God!"

James: "Yeah … well, that's on Mom, not us. I think we're okay.

Peter: "Guys—to be honest with you, I feel a little weak-kneed. I think I'm screwed, and each of you knows why. What all of you have done doesn't even come close to what I've done. At least you guys didn't deny Him. What am I going say to Him? How do I start the conversation? I feel so horrible and shameful. You know He knows … He's the Messiah. He doesn't forget anything!"

Nathanael: "Yeah, you're screwed."

Just then, Jesus called to them, "Come and have some breakfast." The disciples came over and sat down around the burning coals with the delicious fish now ready to serve. Jesus, not unaware of their brief conversations with each other, reached for some bread that he had brought with him and gave some to each of them. As they were eating the bread, Jesus then began to serve them the open fire-cooked fish that He had prepared for them.

NOTE: It's important to see here that Jesus, knowing all the shortcomings of these men, in particular of Peter's, was still being true to His nature and the message that He preached. Etched into the very fiber of who the Messiah was is His message of servitude. *"just* *as the Son of Man did not come to be served, but to serve, and to give his life as a ransom for many."* (Matthew 20:28 NIV) He well understood their human condition, having felt and gone through what they had been subjected to. *"For we do not have a high priest who is unable to empathize with our weaknesses, but we have one who has been <u>tempted in every way</u>, just as we are, yet he did not sin."* (Hebrews 4:15 NIV) The Messiah's love and care, through servitude, both secured the hearts of the disciples while at the same time undoing them.

Who knows what they talked about around the campfire, but this we do know: Jesus eventually began the "Conversation," the conversation that you know Peter was hoping would never happen.

Peter, kind of gathering things around him, maybe even starting to clean up the area a little where he was sitting and eating, hears Jesus say, "So Simon Peter, son of John, do you love me [unconditionally] more than these guys?"

Like someone shooting him in the stomach with a taser, every nerve in Peter's body releases neurotransmitters—communication chemicals to his muscles—that contract like a shocking cramp attack! After a few seconds of this, Peter gathers what's left of his faculties, looks at Jesus, and moves his eyes from one direction to the other and says, "Yes, Lord, You know that I love You. [You're a very dear friend.]"

Jesus then replied to Peter, "[Good then], feed My lambs." Peter's thinking, *What? What did He say? No, I really didn't hear that. Feed my what? Wow, I'm not sure what He's talking about, but I'm sure glad that's over.* Just then, like a rabbit punch, a second time Jesus says to him, "Simon, son of John, [I'm asking you], do you love me [unconditionally]?"

No, not a second time! He can't be asking me this another time, can He? He just asked me this question. Now looking at Jesus a little more connectively, Peter responds, "Yes Lord, [as I said] You know that I love You [like a close and dear friend]."

Then Jesus said back to him, "Then take care of My sheep."

No way! He can't be talking about His followers, can He? Not me taking care of them. I know Him. When He says "sheep" He means those who have received Him and those who have yet to receive Him. This is messed up. I'm a worthless piece of defecation. I'm not worthy of anything like this. This has to be a misunderstanding. Anyway, it's over. Maybe I can get out of here now. It seemed there wasn't a sound being made anywhere. It was almost like the sea and its surroundings went mute while "the conversation" was going on.

Jesus then said a third time, "Simon, son of John, do you love me [like you say, as a very dear and close friend]?"

Then Peter's heart fell, and he became very sad because he knew Jesus was asking him if he loved Him unconditionally just as the Father loves Him and all His creation. But Peter was beating up on himself because he knew that he didn't love Jesus in this way ... He couldn't have because of how he cursed and denied him just less than a month ago. So Peter lifted his head, with tears streaming down his cheeks, and said, "Lord, there's nothing that You don't know. You know all things, even every inch of my heart and every space of my thoughts. Yes, Jesus, I love You dearly as a friend but not unconditionally, not right now, not as a result of what I've done to You. This great sin haunts me. I know I should love You better, but as You know, not now, not yet. I so hate me. You see, Lord, I think that You feel about me the way that I feel about me right now. I've let You down, I fell short of being faithful to You. I'm a failure."

Jesus, with every ounce of love, compassion, and kindness, said to Peter, "I understand Peter, truly I do. It hasn't been, nor will it be, easy to walk this path of unconditional love that the Father and I have for you and for all people. Don't beat yourself up. I know your heart, both the saint side and the dark shadow side. The only thing that I feel toward you, My friend, is love. Yes, Peter, unconditional love. I don't at all think and feel the way that you think and feel about yourself right now. You made a mistake, you sinned, but this is the reason that the Father sent me here, to seek and to rescue those who are lost and fall short of God's commandments. That goes for the one who knows Me and the one who is distant from Me, the one who appears to naturally do the right things in life, and the one who struggles at doing almost anything right in life. These people are going to need you to tell them and teach them what I've told you and taught you. You'll grow from this experience, Peter, and it will help you to be empathetic with those who are in emotional pain and under the enemy's grip of guilt and condemnation. Now come on, stand up. I love you deeply and will always love you no matter how many mistakes you make in life. You've got work to do, now. Feed My sheep, Peter."

Instead of Jesus disqualifying Peter for his sin, He actually commissions him as an apostle to proclaim the gospel of love, redemption, and forgiveness found in the message that the Messiah preached. If only we could catch a glimpse of this great truth with those who we come in contact with on a daily basis…both within and without of the church community. Brennan Manning said, "The gospel of grace calls out: nothing can ever separate you from the LOVE of God made visible in Christ Jesus our Lord. You must be convinced of this, trust it, and never forget to remember. Everything else will pass away, but the LOVE of Christ is the same yesterday, today, and forever. Faith will become vision, hope will become possession, but the love of Jesus Christ that is stronger than death endures forever. In the end, it is the only thing you can hang on to."

What an enormously valuable and spiritual life lesson Jesus was showing Peter and the other disciples about how we're to navigate through our relationship with Him. Also, how we can both be fully dedicated to a holy walk with God and at the same time struggle through our own human brokenness on that walk. God isn't interested so much in a *successful* faith walk as He is in an honest, transparent, and courageous one. If Peter isn't a good example of this, then I don't know anyone who is.

Sir Winston Churchill said, *"Success is not final, failure is not fatal: it is the courage to continue that counts."* Just because we're Christians who serve the Lord doesn't mean that we lose all of our flaws when we dedicate our lives to Him. To the contrary, it's through our flaws and struggles on the journey that we discover the endless love and beautiful grace that God has for all of us in Jesus. Remember, God through His Son specifically came to redeem sinful mankind from the curse of the Fall of Adam. Just in case you missed it, that's "sinful, cursed, fallen mankind." The awareness and benefit of Christ's redemption isn't found in the letter of the Law, but rather in the gift of His grace and the assurance of His love. As painful as it is at times, an intimate and secure relationship with Jesus more often comes out of our human struggle rather than the high places of spiritual bliss.

Being broken isn't something to be ashamed of. It doesn't minimize you or make you a failure. Actually it confirms both your natural susceptibility to life's pain as well as your total dependency on Him who is able to bring life out of death.

"Listen carefully: Unless a grain of wheat is buried in the ground, dead to the world, it is never any more than a grain of wheat. But if it is buried, it sprouts and reproduces itself many times over." —John 12:24 (The Message)

Henri Nouwen put it this way; *"Our life is full of brokenness ... bitter relationships, broken promises, broken expectations. How can we live with that brokenness without becoming bitter and resentful except by returning again and again to God's faithful presence in our lives?* Our human struggle, both in the light and outside of it, makes His presence much more vast than if everything we touched in life turned to gold. Our journey with Christ is found living within both of those dimensions. This is our pathway to God's redemptive definition of just who we are in Christ. If not, then we're daily defined only by the struggle rather than the Savior.

SILENT SUFFERERS

"It's just not the case that faith or religious belief will inoculate or immunize a person against mental illness."

— Rick Warren

The historical mentality of the traditional protestant (evangelical) church toward mental illness has been, for the most part, having a *lack* of faith. It's always pretty much been one-dimensional for many in the church when it comes to a mental health problem, that being a spiritual issue. That amounts to the person who has a mental health illness as (a) having some sort of overt or hidden sin in their life that's causing the problem, (b) the person not demonstrating enough faith to "break through" the problem or (c) the presence of some demonic possession/oppression that is prohibiting the believer from doing life normally.

Within the transdenominational evangelical church throughout the years, the very thought of a believer having a neurological, biological, environmental, chemical, or genetic imbalance that is contributing to the way the person is negatively acting out was biblically unacceptable. Nonetheless, that is exactly what historically

no medication
read Bible

69

has happened. But to be fair, there have been a few rays of hope within the church. For instance, believers from the Mennonite community have been ministering to those with mental illnesses for years. Actually, they were one of the first to provide facilities for those suffering with mental illness.

There have been a variety of Christians and Christian ministries throughout the years who would "care" for those with mental challenges, though very much in the same way someone would care for the sick or diseased. However, having a clinical understanding of mental illness that greatly contributes to a more emotionally stable life was absent. So it's only really been within the last fifty years that we've moved from less of a *care* model to more of a *treatment* model when it comes to helping those with mental illness. It's been in the implementing of the "treatment" (counseling/medication) model that has been the theological challenge for the evangelical church ... in particular the Charismatic wing of the evangelical community.

Sin's Wide Net

When mental illness terms like bipolar, depression, social anxiety, obsessive compulsive disorder (OCD), attention deficit disorder (ADD), posttraumatic stress disorder (PTSD), dissociative identity disorder (DID), just to name a few, are mentioned, the more legalistically minded in the evangelical church throughout the years have theologically flipped out!

In order to get a better perspective of mental health issues, Christianity's and the Bible, we have to go back to the Garden of Eden, the place where all of this human dysfunction began. As I mentioned previously, when Adam fell, it corrupted him in six ways: physically, physiologically, emotionally, neurologically, biologically, and spiritually. If this is true, and I as well as many others believe it is, then let's use a premise here with Cain in Genesis 4:8 where he lured his brother Abel "[into] the field" and killed him.

Sure, we can use the ever familiarly preached reasoning why Cain did this. He was jealous of Abel because God seemed to accept Abel more than he did Cain. Matter of fact, it appears that Cain didn't feel accepted by God at all because verse 4 and 5 says that "[t]he LORD *looked with favor on Abel and his offering, but on Cain and his offering he did not look with favor. So Cain was very angry, and his face was downcast.*" We theologically conclude that the intense jealousy that Cain had regarding the close relationship between Abel and God led to Cain eventually killing his brother.

But think about it. A lot of people get jealous, a lot of people get angry, a lot of people feel slighted or disregarded in relationships, but they don't commit murder as a result of them. For a person to commit murder, something neurologically damaging has to be going on. The most common diagnosis for a murderer is someone who displays *sociopathic* or *psychopathic* traits. Sociopathy is a clinically diagnosed disorder whereby something is severely wrong with a person's conscience and their ability to determine between what is right and wrong. Psychopathy is regarded as a complete lack of conscience regarding others.

These types of people can exhibit a "stone cold" approach to the rights of others. They are often manipulative, lacking in empathy, and violent. This, in my opinion, is where I see Cain. Remember, in verses 6–7 God tried to have the "Why are you angry?" conversation with Cain, but Cain didn't want to hear it. There we see the first sign of his "conscience disregard" for not only his brother, but for God as well. Then, after Cain murdered his brother, we see in verse 9 where God said to Cain, "Where is your brother Abel?" Cain's

Cain — jealousy

reply, "Am I my brother's keeper?" There's his *stone cold* psychopathic response ... to the living God yet!

So what am I saying here? I'm saying that people who murder today as a result of a sociopathic or psychopathic mental health illness are recipients of that disorder because of its origination from Cain. And where did Cain get it from? He caught the sin bug from his dad Adam. It's woven within the far-reaching net of original sin. We see this kind of diagnosis in our society today as a horrifically sick person with a substantial mental illness but somehow think that this illness can't reach within the church. I mean, the First Crusades of 1095 alone were sparked by a sermon by Pope Urban II. We're talking about A LOT of murders here! Yet, there have been other people throughout history who have *killed* in the name of God. Example: Antiabortion protester Paul Hill, on July 29, 1994 in Pensacola, FL, who killed Dr. John Bayard Britton, an abortion doctor and his bodyguard James Barrett. Hill proclaimed to be a Christian yet clearly had a severe mental health issue of psychopathy (abnormal or violent social behavior).

Let's look at a much less dramatic and more common example than the illness that Cain had. Let's view the issue of depression and/ or anxiety within the Body of Christ today. There are a lot of people within the evangelical church who struggle with these two disorders often throughout their life ... in some cases, every day of their lives. In our practice alone, almost daily we counsel people who suffer with some form of depression and/or anxiety. It's about time that this very real issue be addressed within the church.

The World Health Organization reports that depression alone is one of the leading global causes of disabilities, affecting around 121 million people worldwide. It's also important to note that a cousin to depression, anxiety, is the most common mental health issue in the US, affecting 40 million adults in the United States age eighteen and older (18 percent of US population). Anxiety disorders are highly treatable, yet only about one-third of those suffering receive treatment. Mixed within these statistics are some believers in Christ. If you don't get this, then you're going to think that somehow Christians are exempt from depression and anxiety ... and they're not.

From our in-house counseling findings, many Christian believers are reluctant to openly talk with their pastor or another Christian friend about their depression or anxiety because they feel they will be perceived as not having enough *faith* to overcome their problem.

There are two kinds of depression and anxiety: *situational* and *genetic.*

Situational Depression: I seem happy and upbeat and am facing life with hope and optimism. Oops, I went to work on Monday and just found out that my $100,000-a-year job will be terminated in two weeks. I have a wife, two kids, a house payment, two car payments, credit cards, and school tuition. WOW! I've just fallen into a deep depression.

Genetic Depression: I've felt depressed off and on quite a bit throughout my life. Then again, my mom, grandfather, Uncle Charlie, and Aunt Linda suffer from depression as well. Also my great grandfather on my mom's side committed suicide. Now it makes a little more sense why I feel depressed. It's in my lineage.

Situational Anxiety: I took our total savings of $200,000 and invested it in the stock market and have now come to find out that I've lost all but $10,000. The worst part is I never told my wife that I was going to do this, and she knows nothing about the loss of our retirement that took us thirty years to save. I'm having debilitating panic attacks and am highly anxious! Also, situational anxiety may come from a trauma that happened to you as a child or a trauma-related experience such as war, an accident, an abuse, or even an abortion.

Genetic Anxiety: I've always felt apprehensive about things, even troubled. I have this feeling that things in my life just won't work out. It's not uncommon for me to be tense and jumpy and even restless. Sometimes I know why I'm tense, and other times I don't. I worry a lot and my heart at times feels like it's going to beat out of my chest. I get headaches, feel fatigued, and find it difficult to get to sleep or stay asleep. I'm petrified with fear that something bad may happen even though, outwardly, things "appear" okay. Also, there are other relatives on both my mother and father's side who have some of these same symptoms.

These two classes of mental health challenges are very real. They affect people every day. Whether you're not a follower of Jesus or whether you are, the crippling effects of depression and anxiety are present in our society and have been in every society since the fall of Adam.

Paralyzed and Insignificant

A Jesus follower came to me for counseling because of an inability to be able to emotionally connect with opposite sex relationships without feeling overwhelmed by anxiety. The client had a very low opinion of himself and felt that he would sabotage the relationship almost before it started. The client struggled, feeling that his words were not formed right, that he wasn't interesting enough, that he was not bright enough, not confident enough, not spiritual enough, not attractive enough. My client even felt that because he was so indecisive about himself, God had become displeased and angry with him and was going to withhold His blessings and possibly even take my client's life. My client was paralyzed with anxiety as to what to say and how to say it. Is it the right thing to do or is it the wrong thing to do? Am I pleasing God, or is He angry with me? My client's sense of feeling insignificant as a person as well as a Christian in the eyes of God was huge. You might think, *Wow! How could your client think such things about himself not to mention how he could think that God would treat him that way?* Well, now you're beginning to get a glimpse into what obsessive compulsive disorder (OCD) looks like.

On a *theological* level, my client understood that God was love, and that the Word of God clearly spelled out that His plans [are] to "prosper you and not to harm you" (Jeremiah 29:11). However, on a mental and emotional level my client struggled terribly with anxiety. This made my client question the whole "prosper you and not harm you" part of his relationship with God. The sheer fear of living with anxiety as a Christian, for example, can throw a punishing contradiction between your "faith and feelings" when it comes to trying to figure out what God is saying to you in the Bible.

To the well-meaning believer who doesn't struggle with anxiety and is saying to his anxious Christian friend, "Just believe God and stop giving into the devil with all of this anxiety stuff," I would say … "Clearly you've never experienced the horror of anxiety. If you did, you would certainly have much more compassion and empathy for your friend.

Plato rightly said, *"Opinion is the medium between knowledge and ignorance."* Though there may be some truth at times in what we say to the wounded in spirit, when it's all said and done it can be our own arrogance that untimely prohibits any real and genuine healing in them. Jesus was not only the Prince of Peace, He was also the Great Empathizer. *"For we do not have a high priest who is unable to empathize with our weaknesses…"* (Hebrews 4:15).

A mental health disorder is just that, a disorder. It's a disturbance, a dysfunction in the normal activity within a person's brain. The brain is a very complex structure. It contains billions of nerve cells called neurons that must communicate and work together for the body and mind to function normally. If these aren't working well, then anxiety and depression will be present. The brain is the epicenter of where things start for good or bad in us.

After walking through some family history and cognitive behavioral therapy (CBT) with my client, there was an improvement in helping him to stabilize thoughts and obsessive thinking. However, a big factor in stabilization was being placed on a specific antidepressant that was geared more toward an anxiety and OCD disorder than just depression. The result was amazing! My client is now able to use CBT, faith as well as the help of an antidepressant, to keep him more balanced with his low dopamine and serotonin levels. My client was taught that taking antidepressant medication was basically having a "lack of faith." Now with a much better understanding of God's wonderful love and grace along with the knowledge that He has given medical science today, my client is enjoying the experience of an anxiety controlled life! Oh, yeah, and a LOT less guilt and condemnation as well.

Now let's look at the cousin to anxiety, depression. Both are debilitating, but some cases of depression can potentially have a sinister and even deadly twist if not treated.

Depression has a number of faces. Again, situational depression is different, as stated earlier. That's when something has happened that has made you depressed, as an example a job loss or sickness or death in the family. However, clinical depression is when you have depression so severe it's considered abnormal. This is either because of a genetic propensity toward depression or because of unfortunate life circumstances that are more intense or prolonged than would generally be expected. And yes, Christians can and do experience this form of depression. For those who do, you're not a weak Christian because you've experienced this, and you don't have a third eye in the middle of your forehead. A lot of Christians have depression, and there is real help for those who do.

The most common type of depression is Major Depressive Disorder, which is also known as clinical depression. This kind of depression is recognized by a combination of symptoms that interfere with a person's ability to sleep, work, study, eat, and enjoy any pleasurable activities. This form of depression often makes it hard for a person to do much of anything or even get motivated.

Let's look at one famous Bible character who suffered with bouts of depression throughout his whole adult life.

King David

David's story is one of the most dramatic stories in the Bible. His life was a series of highs and lows. Also, David's leadership decision making wasn't exactly the best. Still he was labeled "a man after God's own heart" (Acts 13:22). The main reason David earned that title was because he was always remorseful for his sins. Even in his dysfunction and sin, David had a heart that longed deeply for God, not unlike us. I mean, think about it. David committed adultery with his officer's wife (Bathsheba), got her pregnant, and then brought her husband (Uriah) from the battlefield to come home and spend some time with his wife so it would look like Uriah was the dad and not David. When that didn't work out, David then instructed one of his generals to place Uriah on the front lines of the battlefield where it was the most dangerous, almost assuring Uriah's death. In essence,

David had Uriah bumped off...murdered! This alone is enough evidence to throw David into the sociopathic category. David also appears to have suffered from depression, possibly even a type of bipolar depression. Listen to him cry out to God, in what seems to be, at times, emotional torment.

"Save me, O God, for the waters have come up to my neck. I sink in the miry depths, where there is no foothold. I have come into the deep waters; the floods engulf me. I am worn out calling for help; my throat is parched. My eyes fail, looking for my God."

—Psalm 69:1–3

"LORD, do not rebuke me in your anger or discipline me in your wrath. Your arrows have pierced me, and your hand has come down on me. Because of your wrath there is no health in my body; there is no soundness in my bones because of my sin. My guilt has overwhelmed me like a burden too heavy to bear. My wounds fester and are loathsome because of my sinful folly. I am bowed down and brought very low; all day long I go about mourning. My back is filled with searing pain; there is no health in my body. I am feeble and utterly crushed; I groan in anguish of heart."

—Psalm 35:1–8

This was no light thing going on here with David. Let's face it, he was one messed up mental health case. Yet he loved God with all of his heart...and God loved him right back. And isn't it interesting, because with great reverence and piety we quote this man of God endlessly with little to no regard as someone with a possible mental health disorder. Not that this should make a difference. By virtue of David's weakness as a struggling believer in God, we can then empathize with him when it comes to our struggle with depression. We connect so often with David because of the great contradictions in his life. He was strong while being weak. He had a vibrant faith in God yet struggled with keeping God's commandments. He had many talents and great leadership skills, yet battled constantly with his numerous human flaws. He was both a victorious and gallant warrior as well as an emotionally troubled and controversial failure. David was forgiven by God for the sins and yet struggled with feeling forgiven. Wow! Give or take a few things, it sounds like many of us.

In the Company of Giants:
Martin Luther (1483-1546)

Martin Luther was a German monk, priest, professor of theology, and the main influential figure of the Protestant Reformation. This great man of God also struggled with major depression. There are psychologists who actually believe Luther's writings reveal someone who may have had a bipolar disorder. Luther described his mental health disorder in varied terms: melancholy, heaviness, depression, dejection of spirit; downcast, sad, and downhearted. He suffered in this area for much of his life and often revealed these struggles in his works. Clearly, Luther didn't think it a shameful problem to be hidden. Besides personally being depressed, Luther was also known to observe mental difficulties in others as well.

Luther's writings reveal his knowledge of various emotional difficulties. For example, in August 1536 he interceded for a woman named Mrs. Kreuzbinder, who he felt was insane. He described her as being "accustomed to rage" and sometimes angrily chasing her neighbor with a spear. In addition, Luther's wife, Kate, struggled with pervasive and persistent worry, a symptom of generalized anxiety disorder. Prince Joachim of Anhalt, to whom Luther often wrote, exhibited signs of obsessive compulsive disorder, and he believed he had betrayed and crucified Christ. Conrad Cordatus, a pastor and frequent guest at Luther's table, exhibited signs of hypochondriasis, a disorder involving preoccupation with fears of having a serious disease.

Luther also recognized that depression runs in families (what we call *family systems* today). He saw this trend in the brothers Jerome and Matthias Weller. Likewise Luther saw similar family links in some royalty. In his letter to Prince Joachim, Luther noted that other members of his family had been "...of a retiring, quiet, and sober nature." He then used those family traits to conclude that Prince Joachim's illness derived from "melancholy and dejection of spirit." He implied that other members of the family had struggled in this area as well.

Because of Luther's depression, he used a number of means to try to combat it for not only him, but for others as well. Some ways he suggested lessening depression were prayer, the reading of scripture, other believer's praying for the depressed, and using "*joking, jesting and enjoying other forms of merriment*" as a means of help. Another means that Luther used to lessen the effects of his depression was beer. Martin Luther was a very fond beer and wine lover. Luther wrote about beer in several of his letters, at one point writing to tell his wife (Katharina) how much he missed the beer they brewed at home. "I keep thinking what good wine and beer I have at home, as well as a beautiful wife ....You would do well to send me over my whole cellar of wine and a bottle of thy beer." The problem, though, was that because of Luther's depression, he would self-medicate from too much of that beer and wine to ease the heaviness. Apparently Luther was well known for his consumption of beer. Luther said, "*We old folks have to find our cushions and pillows in our tankards. Strong beer is the milk of the old.*" The problem was Luther appears to have abused this liberty, no doubt because of his mood disorder. If only antidepressants were available at that time, perhaps good old Martin Luther wouldn't have sucked down so much suds!

Charles Spurgeon (1834-1892)

Charles Spurgeon was a famous pastor in England who spoke to over 10 million people in his lifetime. Spurgeon would often speak from the pulpit up to ten times a week. Spurgeon was known, and still is, as the Prince of Preachers. He is the author of numerous books, many still in print today.

Aside from the powerful things he did for the Gospel and the understanding of theology, what we should also know is that Spurgeon suffered from depression. One Sunday morning in 1866, from the pulpit of his London Metropolitan Tabernacle, he shocked his congregation of 5,000 by admitting, *"I am the subject of depressions of spirit so fearful that I hope none of you ever gets to such extremes of wretchedness as I go to."* He later described his depression as a *"seething caldron of despair."* He spoke of his depression in his article as, "lowness of spirit" and "thick darkness." Here are some direct quotes from Spurgeon himself regarding his depressive mental health disorder.

"I could weep by the hour like a child, and yet I knew not what I wept for."

"The iron bolt ... mysteriously fastens the door of hope and holds our spirits in gloomy prison. I have sometimes been the means in God's hand of healing a man who suffered with a desponding spirit. But the help I have rendered has cost me dearly. Hours after, I have been myself depressed, and I have felt an inability to shake it off."

"I am the subject of depression so fearful that I hope none of you ever get to such extremes of wretchedness as I go to. But I always get back again by this—I know that I trust Christ. I have no reliance but in Him, and if He falls, I shall fall with Him. But if He does not, I shall not. Because He lives, I shall live also, and I spring to my legs again and fight with my depressions of spirit and get the victory through it. And so may you do, and so you must, for there is no other way of escaping from it."

"We have our times of natural sadness; we have, too, our times of depression, when we cannot do otherwise than hang our heads. Seasons of lethargy will also befall us from changes in our natural frame, or from weariness, or the rebound of overexcitement. The trees are not always green, the sap sleeps in them in the winter; and we have winters too. Life cannot always be at flood tide: the fullness of the blessing is not upon the most gracious at all times. I often feel very grateful to God that I have undergone fearful depression of spirits. I know the borders of despair and the horrible brink of that gulf of darkness into which my feet have almost gone, but hundreds of times I have been able to give a helpful grip to brethren and sisters who have come into that same condition, which grip I could never have given if I had not known their deep despondency. So I believe that the darkest and most dreadful experience of a child of God will help him to be a fisher of men if he will but follow Christ."

So, here you have it, the great theologian Charles Spurgeon, just another example of a great Christian who struggled with clinical depression and possibly even a mood disorder, a struggler, yet a lover of Christ.

John Wesley (1703-1791)

Today, what John Wesley called "Lowness of Spirits" would be better known as depression, which is classified as a mood disorder in the DSM-V for mental health diagnosis. Wesley described this "lowness" as follows;

"We sometimes say, 'A man is in high spirits,' and the proper opposite to this is, 'He is low spirited.' Does not this imply that a kind of faintness, weariness, and listlessness affects the whole body, so that he is disinclined to any motion, and hardly cares to move hand or foot? But the mind seems chiefly to be affected, having lost its relish of everything, and being no longer capable of enjoying the things it once delighted in most. Nay, everything round about is not only flat and insipid, but dreary and uncomfortable. It is not strange if, to one in this state, life itself is become a burden; yea, so insupportable a burden, that many who have all this world can give, desperately rush into an unknown world, rather than bear it any longer."

Some of Wesley's journals are marked by mention of his depression. When he came back from America after trying to convert the Indians, it was said that Wesley was *"a disheartened and depressed man."* Also comments that he was *"still in a very unsettled state of mind, alternately exalted and depressed."* (*John Wesley: A Personal Portrait* by Ralph Waller)

Wesley's *The Holy Club* at Oxford was well known for visiting prisons. In Wesley's day, both he and his brother Charles would visit prisons in England as well as in America. Often those with mental illness are found in prisons for a multitude of reasons, but like Jesus, John and Charles Wesley were no strangers to mental illness. It was something that John Wesley faced often in his ministry with others, and there were even times he faced it himself.

Ashbel Green (1762–1848)

Ashbel Green, D.D. was an American Presbyterian minister and academic. Born in Hanover Township, New Jersey, Green served as a sergeant of the New Jersey militia during the American Revolutionary War.

Ashbell Green was also someone who suffered from depression, or as he called it, "his bouts with melancholy." Here are some quotes from Green regarding his sufferings with depression.

"My melancholy consisted in a settled gloom of mind, accompanied with spiritual difficulties of the most distressing character." (*The Life of Ashbel Green*, 301–302)

In his *Lectures on the Shorter Catechism*, Green goes into more detail about the "peculiar character of my spiritual difficulties and temptations." Notice both the presence of anxiety as well as depression in his writing.

Mother Teresa (1910-1997)

Mother Teresa was a Roman Catholic religious sister and missionary who lived most of her life in India. Mother Teresa founded the Missionaries of Charity, a Roman Catholic religious congregation, which in 2012 consisted of over 4,500 sisters and is active in 133 countries. They run hospices and homes for people with HIV/AIDS, leprosy, and tuberculosis. They run soup kitchens, dispensaries and mobile clinics, children's and family counseling programs, orphanages, and schools.

Through all of her many kindnesses, deep love for Jesus, and humanitarian help to the sick and underprivileged, even this couldn't stop the flood of depression that would come over her at times. In her own words...

Mother Teresa wrote in September of 1959; "If I ever become a saint—I will surely be one of 'darkness.' I will continually be absent from heaven—to light the light of those in darkness on earth." *thorn in the flesh by satan*

Two years earlier she wrote this to Archbishop Perier of Calcutta: "There is so much contradiction in my soul—such deep longing for God—so deep that it is painful—a suffering continual—and yet not wanted by God—repulsed—empty—no faith—no love—no zeal. Souls hold no attraction—Heaven means nothing—to me it looks like an empty place—the thought of it means nothing to me and yet this torturing longing for God. Pray for me please that I keep smiling at Him in spite of everything. For I am only His—so He has every right over me. I am perfectly happy to be nobody even to God."

In a compilation entitled "Come Be My Light," edited by Brian Kolodiejchuk, M.C., Mother Teresa was quoted as saying...

"And I wept many times throughout the book, mostly at her graciousness toward God in her suffering. I want to smile even at Jesus and so hide if possible the pain and the darkness of my soul even from Him."

Mother Teresa depressed? Come on, no way! Could this faithful woman of God be plagued with doubt and mental despair? But yet it's true, she and all of the rest who have been mentioned and the untold millions throughout the years who cannot be mentioned. Depression, anxiety, etc., are no newcomers to the church.

Jill's Story

Jill was a former Amish-raised young lady who came into my office upon the request of those who loved her most, her family. Actually, I believe the last thing that Jill wanted was to come into my office for counseling...she as much as told me that. But because of years of depression, agitation, anxiety, and mood swings, Jill said yes, that she would try counseling and made an appointment to see me. The first session was uncomfortable for Jill. We moved through the normal client intake info and made an attempt at getting to the reason why Jill had come in. After a little while of guiding her through some, "try to make you feel more comfortable" conversation, I asked the question. "So, Jill, what brings you here today?"

With a clear voice and a straight forward look, the kind of look that says, "Where am I at?" Jill said, "I'm here because my family thinks I'm crazy."

I said, "Well, what do you think?"

She came right back with, "Yeah, I probably am."

The first session was moving and dancing around some of the outside issues that were, in some way, protecting the major issue that brought Jill in. Jill was cautious and peripheral with her answers and responses that first session. I would ask a question. Jill would respond with a "yes or "no" answer. At times she would build on a question asked, but ever so cautiously. She would try to frame her answers just right so as not to divulge too much information too soon. Also, there was a part of Jill that wasn't even sure where to go with some of the questions. Guarded, vague, and emotionally fatigued, we began to get to the heart of her issue.

From ages two to fourteen, Jill was sexually molested by four of her brothers on their Amish farm. Jill carried with her the trauma from this horrendous offense all of her life. Because of the nature of the trauma, Jill suppressed her feelings, not wanting to come to grips with just how all of this has affected her. The guilt and shame that she experienced was so overpowering that she learned early on that the only way she could possibly cope with such horror was to *suppress* her feelings. So, that's exactly what she did. Days after weeks after months after years Jill buried her pain and trauma until it was so deep she thought she may have buried it deep enough to no longer feel. The problem is there is no hole deep enough that can bury such devastating and wounding pain. The quiet, shame, self-condemnation, and emotional trauma took its toll on Jill throughout the years. She had become angry, depressed, anxious, and very moody. Unknowingly to Jill, the trauma was adversely affecting every area of her life, from her marriage to her parenting to her spiritual life to her emotional stability. Nothing was off limits to the systemic effect of her pain.

Because of the potential family complications of the trauma, Jill left the Amish community when she was nineteen, never to return again. Her husband also left and together they attempted to carve out a life as "English." As a result of Jill leaving the Amish faith (after having been baptized), she was and remains now shunned by her family and those in her former Amish community. The rejection and religious abuse of this action has been painfully substantial to Jill. But again, she taught herself early on to bury her pain. Burying her pain she continued to do, deeper and deeper until her memories formed a numbing glaze over them suitable enough to at least partially get by each day. Aside from this, her mother and father to this day do not know the abuse that their sons have done to their daughter. Rather than cause any further pain in her family, in particular to her parents, Jill just took the cruel lashes of rejection and abandonment and tearfully moved on. Jill was suffering, and not at all suffering well.

Jill told me that she remembers on her honeymoon standing out on the deck of their cruise ship gazing down into the calm sea from the ship's railing as she heard the splashing of the waves up against the large cruise liner. She thought, *I could jump over this railing and drown myself.* The urging of that thought was becoming larger in her head, until the actual thought of committing suicide was becoming much more of a reality. Between the sound of the sea splashing against the ship, the stillness of the night, and the fact that no one was in proximity made the thought even more inviting. The atmosphere was fearfully mesmerizing. The voice in her head became louder ... JUMP! JUMP! Just then, she remembered hearing someone from a distance *cough*. For some reason, she said, that sound snapped her back into reality and broke her dangerous obsessive thinking pattern. It wasn't until she told this story in session that she came to realize the cough that she heard was either a person that God moved upon to cough so that Jill could hear them, or, perhaps God Himself made the noise of a human cough in order to break the death trance that the enemy had on Jill. Either way, God clearly intervened to spare Jill from apparent suicide.

NOTE: Cases like Jill's often form into what is known as dissociative identity disorder (DID), formerly known as multiple personality disorder. In the past, I've counseled DID patients who were sexually molested by fewer people and within a shorter span of time. However, this was the first time I had ever encountered such a long span of molestation on a person by family members (four brothers) that ended up *not* becoming DID. It was both clinically and spiritually amazing!

After some sessions, Jill became desperate for healing and wanted to see God set her free from the years of emotional pain and tortured thoughts. Actually, that was one of her key questions to me, *"Can I ever be really free of these memories and pain?"* I said "Yes, you can!" So we started to get to work. The bottom line for legitimate healing to any offense, including sexual abuse, is eventually forgiveness. We must work to a place of forgiveness because if not, the victim will always be imprisoned by the offender both physiologically and emotionally. Forgiveness is beautifully and effectively designed by God to release us from the anger, resentment, and injustice that dreadfully places itself on us throughout our human struggle. Jesus talked about forgiveness a lot in the Gospels. But one of the most impactful statements He made regarding forgiveness is found in Matthew 6:12, in what is known as the Lord's Prayer. *"Forgive us for the wrong things we have done, the way we forgive those who have done wrong things to us."* (*Worldwide English New Testament*)

Forty-one years in the ministry have convinced me that many believers have little understanding of what the enormous and far-reaching power of forgiveness can accomplish in a person. Where there is not the granting of genuine Jesus forgiveness, there remains the presence of anger and resentment. These two forces coupled up have the potential of emotionally, relationally, and spiritually crippling a person depending on the offence done to them. We as followers of Christ "theologically" understand that we're to forgive. We have no problem with the biblical concept, acceptance, and reasoning behind forgiveness. That part we get. Here's the challenge though. We clearly know that we *are* to forgive, but we just don't know *how* to forgive.

A few things forgiveness is not. It isn't *forgetting* (whatever that means), and it isn't *excusing* the person who has wronged you. The temporal lobes of the human brain are designed for memory recall, leaving images, conversations, and experiences lodged within us throughout our lives. We don't usually forget major impacting events in our lives. Where there is a negative or harmful event that has caused trauma or anger, it can revisit us often when remembered or triggered. It's kind of like the event happening over and over again throughout the years. Going to a place of forgiveness greatly minimizes if not rids a person of the painful and emotionally charged memories of the offense. Why? Forgiveness is specifically designed by God through Christ to potentially eliminate all damaging anger and resentment in a person from a wrong[s] suffered. If we don't empty unforgiveness from our heart, then the enemy becomes successful by "defining" us throughout our lives by those two destructive foes, *anger* and *resentment*. Therefore, we end up, even unknowingly at times, taking on the identity of those two damaging forces. Moving to a place where you have forgiven a wrong suffered actually frees you of the many complicated emotional and life relational tentacles attached to that wrong. If we don't, then life and its many facets may not end up being a pleasant experience at all.

So Jill, though at first understandably reluctant, decided to face her painful past and move to a place of forgiveness. Originally the mere thought of forgiving her brothers for such an atrocity wasn't something she cared to think about. But as Jill became more aware of just what forgiveness was and was not, and the great potential for good it could have on her, she then became more open. Jill worked very hard in sessions, at times feeling like she would take one step forward and then two steps backward. Working with someone who has PTSD from sexual trauma takes time and patience. Professional clinical skills are needed and very helpful, but reliance on the power of the Holy Spirit for timing in such cases is absolutely essential.

Because of Jill's love for Christ and the sheer tenacity God put in her as a human being, she has moved from being paralyzed and defined by her anger and emotional pain to a place of hope, freedom, and endless possibilities. She is relationally and spiritually connecting deeper with her husband, her children, and their local church. Jill has finally forgiven her brothers who sexually abused her and is moving forward with her life and her faith, more free from the grip of shame, guilt, anger, and resentment than she has ever experienced. Her trauma will never be completely erased from her brain, but Jill is determined to move and live in the person that God has always *originally* designed her to be rather than what the enemy had been trying to redefine her as.

The wonderfully redeeming part of God, us, and mental health issues is that His Son Jesus "got it!" He completely comprehended and understood the depravity and fallen nature of corrupted mortal flesh. It was the reason He came, the purpose behind Him being the Messiah.

For many years in the evangelical church, too often the emotionally suffering have felt that silence is a more comforting protection than possibly their own pastor or elder[s]. I don't mean to paint with a broad brush here because certainly this doesn't apply in all cases. But it has applied, and still does, in more cases than should be. When you show empathy toward others, their wall of defense and fear comes down and, as a result, they feel safer talking to you. The agape love of God then replaces guilt and condemnation, and that's when the life of Jesus breaks through to a place of answers and progress. It's not difficult. It just requires an honest and introspective look at how we deal with and treat people. Treating people and loving them just as we would like to be treated and loved ... imagine that!

5

WHEN SCARS BECOME YOUR FRIEND

"Out of suffering have emerged the strongest souls; the most massive characters are seared with scars."

— <u>Khalil Gibran</u>

I remember when I was seven years old throwing a baseball back and forth with my older brother Albert in the living room of our small row house in Baltimore, Maryland. For some reason, that little row house looked a whole lot bigger when I was seven than it did when I would visit it as an adult. Those who have been raised in row homes know what I'm talking about. My brother was at the end of our small living room, and I was backed up close to the front of the storm glass window door.

Back and forth the baseball went until the inevitable happened. My brother threw a high-speed zinger at me and I missed the ball, which propelled right through the glass door. Yeah, I know we shouldn't have been playing fast pitch baseball in the living room of such a small row house, but hey, what can I say? We were young and stupid. Crash! Glass flew everywhere! Aside from being shocked by the ball going through the glass door, I thought, *Wow, Mom's gonna kill us when she finds out!*

As we both stood there looking at the glass all over the place and gazing through the big jagged glass hole in the storm door, I couldn't help noticing that the baseball was just on the other side of the glass outside of the door on the porch. It was well within reaching distance for me to get. In just a split second I thought, *Hey, I can get that baseball by just reaching through this big hole in the glass and picking it up.* Being the bright and highly intelligent seven-year-old that I was, I reached with my left arm through the jagged glass hole. As a result, I cut my upper forearm on a sharp piece of glass that was sticking down, leaving me with a two-inch long deep gash. Actually I didn't even feel the glass cut me. It wasn't until I noticed blood running down my arm and onto the floor that I finally understood what had happened.

Running in circles around the living room screaming and totally freaking out (I'm ADHD) brought my mom running down the steps (yep, *running* down the steps) from her upstairs bedroom. When she noticed all of the blood on my arm and on the floor, now we had two people running around in circles freaking out (yeah, she was ADHD too)! Two freaked out people, and I'm bleeding to death!

After she finally pulled herself together, Mom wrapped my arm up with two towels and then rushed me to the doctor's office (that's when you could still walk into a doctor's office with these kind of emergencies). The doctor then proceeded to clean me up, numb me up, and then clamped me up. That's right, rather than suturing my arm, which he actually should have done, he ended up clamping it instead with five wound clamps. When the wound finally healed, the result of this procedure left a scar the size of the tattoo on Popeye's big arm. Suturing it would have left a much thinner and less conspicuous scar.

Here's the takeaway that I received from that self-induced childhood trauma of mine. Eventually the bleeding stopped, the pain stopped, and the scar healed up very well. I've had it all of these years, and it's never bothered me again. But here's the thing: …to this very day, any time I see one of those panel trucks with glass strapped to the side of them riding down the road or highway, I make it a point to quickly pass them. I don't want to be anywhere near those glass trucks! It's just a healthy respect (fear) I still carry from the memory of that childhood trauma. You see, the very thing that hurt me as a child has actually ended up being my friend throughout the years. Anytime I've had to replace a pane of glass or I'm even around glass, I'm very, very cautious…like surgically cautious! Why? I don't ever want to repeat that same mistake and experience again if I can at all help it.

The Beauty of Mistakes and Failures

Johnny Cash said, *"You build on failure. You use it as a stepping stone. You don't try to forget the mistakes, but you don't dwell on them either."* No one can go through life without making mistakes or failing. As much as we evangelical believers in Jesus may try, we're going to come up short at times from hitting the mark. That's just the way life is and, I might add, the way it should be. The mistakes and failures that we experience on the journey can actually become the portals of discovery that lay the groundwork for a no repeat in our life. Scars from past mistakes can actually be your friend when you encounter them again with a potential failure. don't ostracize

Saul of Tarsus had been such a vicious persecutor of Christians that or even after his conversion the brethren were still afraid of him. After he came to Christ and after some time of discipleship, Paul eventually returned to Jerusalem. Barnabas had to persuade the other apostles to

count yourself out of the ballgame. You may have lost a game but shoot for the championship legalism — no acceptance of failure

Straight mistakes are opportunities + positive challenges

A's rigid over-confident Consol

fellowship with Paul after talking to them about his new conversion at Damascus (Acts 9:27). As a result of Barnabas going to bat for Paul, a close friendship between the two was formed. Because of this, it's rather sad to note that these two strong Christian leaders eventually had a "falling out" of sorts. Paul didn't want to take Barnabas' cousin John Mark back with them on their second missionary journey because he "deserted them in Pamphylia" (Acts 15:38). Barnabas wanted John Mark to go with them. Paul and Barnabas both went back and forth with this until in (Acts 15:39) it says, *"They had such a sharp disagreement that they parted company,"* two pretty strong-willed men, neither one allowing the other to budge him.

We don't hear about these two men of God being together again until (Galatians 2) when several years later Paul meets up with Barnabas, and they once again join forces at the Jerusalem conference to champion the cause of a law-free mission to the Gentiles. We're just left to assume that the two must have made peace with each other as they worked in ministry toward a common good.

Some might see the lack of flexibility and stubbornness between these two men as not showing true humility and therefore not moving in genuine Jesus agape love. There arguably may be a case for that. But even if this exists, their failure to get it right in (Acts 15) seems to have worked better for them in (Galatians 2). I'd like to think that the differences that they had in their dispute over John Mark were settled on their coming together at that Jerusalem conference. Hopefully their earlier failure as younger, idealistic Christian leaders who drove that "sharp disagreement" ended by looking through those portals of discovery that laid the groundwork for a future no-repeat. That's what mistakes and failures are good for. If not, then they're good for nothing.

Not a whole lot has really changed that much since Paul and Barnabas. We've all had moments like this, some more vigorously than others, depending on your temperament. The greatest moments in our lives though are when we do make mistakes and learn from them. That's the beauty of mistakes...a second chance to do it right. That's when they end up strangely becoming your friend rather than your foe. It's only when you have allowed the enemy to convince you that your failure is final are you then finally a failure.

Pain, Sorrow and Suffering

If you're really honest, whether it's pain, sorrow, suffering, or all three, many of us, if not all of us, have experienced the sad encounter of this feared, three-headed beast at some time in our lives.

In the first chapter, I shared about the relational complications of having an emotional affair. I say *emotional affair* because I personally have seen more individual and relational damage done in this type of affair than in a "one-night stand." The emotional affair can be potentially much longer and the connection much stronger between the two.

A married client came to me from out of state and began to share with me his story of entering into an emotional affair with a woman in his church. As a crisis marriage therapist, I've heard these kind of stories many times before. But this story, though having a familiar theme, was different. As the man began to open up with me, he shared how this encounter was the first time anything like this had ever happened to him in his marital life. He was a respected businessman who loved his wife, was a father, pillar in his community, elder in his church, and had been a Christian for many years. He said that the "other woman" was also a good person and nothing like this had ever happened to her as well.

It started out as casual glances to one another as they sat in church. Then it would be very brief conversations in the hall of the church building. Finally they met to talk. From there it just escalated, not into a sexual affair, but a deep emotionally bonding affair. As the man went on to share his story, he would break down from time to time with such intensely painful and heart-wrenching crying that I even found myself tearing up with him at times. He said that his sorrow was a combination of both the "sad pain and distance" that it now placed between him and his wife and also the "deep unbelievably painful loss" of the other woman that he knew he could have nothing to do with. He described his experience as being "blindsided" by the enemy. He said that connecting with this lady was not anything that he had planned, and that though he could tell he was being attracted to this person, it was very subtle. He tried hard to pay little attention to it, but he said that it was bigger than he was. Before he knew it, he was sucked in by his own devices. He said the feelings were mutual by the other woman.

His pain, sorrow, suffering, and grief were probably the worst that I had ever seen in a person who had an emotional affair. The residual life effect of his affair lasted for several years. We had talked about "scars" and how they stay with all of us throughout our lives, but what is it that we learn from them in the end? His experience has now schooled him to be very cautious and on the lookout for "sneak-ups." His years of pain have actually drawn him closer and more dependent on the Lord, not just in these types of situations but in multiple other areas of his life. My client has tasted the waters of a deeper well regarding the grace and agape of God in his life. He was cut to the quick, but now the scar of that wound has become the friend that reminds him of what he cannot encounter again.

The Divorce Scar

It seems more and more in our counseling practice we see a number of people who either have been divorced or are on the verge of being divorced. And just to be clear, at least 90 percent of individuals and couples coming to us are Christians. However, the stats are interesting when you look at them.

Sure we wish the statistics on divorce were much lower (presently 45 percent to 50 percent), and yes, there is an enormous attack on marriages today. But the big question should be: how are we going to minister and love these broken souls to a place of healing in the Body of Christ? This doesn't mean we're embracing or condoning divorce or cohabitation, but it is acknowledging it exists just like acknowledging depression, moral failure, sexual addiction, obesity, drug abuse, and other disorders exist in the church. We all wish that none of this were happening, but it is. So because it is, how are we going to approach this issue and extend the life of Jesus to these struggling souls? Do we as Jesus followers cut them out of our lives because they made a mistake or now find themselves in a divorce situation that perhaps they didn't ask for, or do we extend the agape of God and His grace to them as we help them walk out of their painful struggle and hopefully into a better place as they journey with the Lord?

Chris Easterly powerfully brings out in the Samaritan woman's convoluted sexual condition that "Jesus chose [even] her to spread His message" when it says, in John 4:39, *"Many of the Samaritans from that town believed in him because of the woman's testimony."*

Now, I make no claims at all of being the most knowledgeable theologian, but if Jesus can use a woman having five former husbands and presently living with a man in sin to spread His Good News to a whole town, then He clearly can forgive the adulterer referred to in Matthew 19:9. If you don't think so, then try this on. In Matthew 5:28, Jesus makes another bold statement. He said, *"But I tell you that anyone who looks at a woman lustfully has already committed adultery with her in his heart."* Okay then, is God able to forgive the sin of lust if you ask Him to? But aren't you, according to what Jesus said, committing adultery in your heart (soul/mind)? And if a man or woman looks at pornography, isn't that also, according to what Jesus said, committing adultery in his/ her heart as well?

For the divorcée in the church who has silently suffered throughout the years and has worn the scarlet stain of falling short, be encouraged. Jesus can proclaim the Good News to the captives through you! But before you can do that, you must first set yourself free from the stigma and condemnation of feeling "less than" in the eyes of God. Even your pain of divorce can be a friendly scar of wisdom for future relationships.

Yes, at all costs try to repair a fractured marriage. Do all that you can through all means that you can. But, if in the end, divorce does happen, and to think somehow that there is no forgiveness for you is then to say there is no redemption provided for any of us when it comes to falling short.

There are many scars (mistakes) that can end up being our friend. Adultery, deception, cheating, saying things we wish we hadn't said, hurting a friend, making a bad business move, going bankrupt, etc. John Powell said, *"The only real mistake is the one from which we learn nothing."* So we take the negative that the enemy wants to define us by and, by the grace of God, turn it into a "life positive." Mistakes...that's the reason they put erasers on the ends of pencils, and so does God erase them with you as well...to start over for a "no repeat."

6

THE POWER OF FORGIVENESS

"We must develop and maintain the capacity to forgive. He who is devoid of the power to forgive is devoid of the power to love. There is some good in the worst of us and some evil in the best of us."

— Dr. Martin Luther King

A couple came to me for marital counseling. The major issue was with the husband. The wife—let's call her Rhonda—said that her husband—let's call him Tim—was and had been, throughout their marriage, very angry, critical, impatient, verbally abusive at times, and unwilling to see his own shortcomings. They had been married for thirty-five years.

Throughout the years, Ronda had developed a resentment and anger toward Tim that now had reached a boiling point. His constant put-downs, demeaning nature, and inability to empathize with both Rhonda and the kids slowly but surely caused them to build a wall of protection between them.

Rhonda had had enough. The last five years had taken a particular toll on her because of the pressure she was under having to caregive for her ill mother who needed almost constant attention. They did have a nurse who was at the house caring for her mom half of the day. Though this was helpful to Rhonda, still she had ongoing responsibilities with her mom, plus trying to maintain the household, navigate three teenagers, and hold down a part-time job.

Tim felt that working 40 hours a week and giving Rhonda the paycheck was enough for him to do in fulfilling his family responsibilities. Oh, yeah, there was the lawn that he took care of and the dogs that he fed (and showed affection to) so tack that on as well. One of the children said, "I wish I were a blade of grass or a lab dog because if I were, I'd get attention and affection from Dad." Mom was almost nonstop working and care-giving with little to no help from Tim. The kids were in desperate need of their father's guidance, care and, affection, but Tim was AWOL as both a dad and a husband. On top of this, there was his critical, moody, inability to empathize, agitated, angry at times ways that the family had to constantly dance around. Needless to say, life wasn't hearts and flowers in this family dynamic.

After thirty-five years of this, Rhonda finally got fed up and wanted out of the marriage. You could hear it in her comments, and you could see it in her eyes. It's what we call here in our counseling practice, "Elvis has left the building!" She was GONE! This is when the abused—Rhonda in this case—had finally come to the emotional conclusion that after thirty-five years of being treated in this way, she was done with the abuser—in this case Tim.

We met for another couple session with Rhonda in this state of mind regarding Tim. She wanted out. She said she was through and wanted to now begin to prepare Tim for life without her. Tim, on the other hand, was now remorseful and was doing everything he could to meet Rhonda's needs. Everything that Rhonda had wanted from Tim for thirty-five years—attention, affection, patience, consideration, and feeling valued—she was resenting even more because now that she's ready to walk out the door, Tim decides to give it to her. She felt used and taken for granted, and she was looking for the door. Tim was freaking out at the thought of life without Rhonda. He was just now beginning to see all that she meant to him and all that she had to put up with when it came to him and his actions throughout the years.

I talked to Rhonda about trusting God for a *genesis* to happen between Tim and her. This is when the abused enters into a time of reflection, determination and prayer, and makes a decision to trust God to "create" a love that has been lost for the abuser. This approach takes a very concerted effort on the part of the abuser to treat the abused in a way that he/she has always wanted to be treated while at the same time realizing that they must be very patient while doing so. In other words, the abuser must give the abused something that the abuser will find very hard to give them ... TIME! It took thirty-five years for Rhonda to get to where she was, and it's not going to take two weeks of Tim doing the right things for her to snap her out of it. The TIME thing is often the challenge for the abuser. Sooner is better for them but, for the abused, it's the complete opposite. If Tim wasn't willing to allow Rhonda to walk through her anger and resentment toward him—at her pace—then any hope of a genesis for this marriage would be futile. In this case Tim said that he would, and Rhonda said that she would try.

Because of the vast dead lands of history that existed in this marriage, we had to start anew. In marital cases like this where there is so much resentment, anger, and historical wounding, I start with the only word that can even remotely have any hope of bringing restoration to the marriage ... FORGIVENESS. Traditionally the abuser, in these cases, is more willing to forgive and move on. However, the abused is reluctant. At this time, forgiving Tim was the

closes you off
shuts down your spirit - deflates
feel justified

last thing that Rhonda wanted to do, and I completely understood her reservations.

Forgiveness is a double-edged sword. On one side it provides the possibility of healing that will lead to a restorative new beginning. On the other side, there is this reservation that says, *It isn't fair that after thirty-five years of relational abuse, I now have to forgive Tim without him feeling any of the pain and rejection that he caused me and the children.* I get it. It makes human sense, and empathizing with a person here is helpful. But unless we look to the words of Jesus when it comes to restoring broken and angry relationships, then we're just going to be treating a cancer with a Band-Aid when it comes to our life with others who have hurt us. Rhonda decided that she would at least try. So we began the long road to a more life-giving and forgiving marriage.

The Jesus Way

Of all the world's religions, only Christianity offers complete forgiveness. To offer forgiveness takes the implementation of two forces that man struggles with more than any other, *love* and *humility*. Actually, Jesus showed us an example of all three on the cross—love, humility, and forgiveness. His very purpose in coming to earth for us was motivated out of (agape) love. The act of dying the type of barbaric and degrading death that He did was an act of humiliation in and of itself. The plan between Him and the Father from the inception was to forgive mankind and set it free from the death grip stemming from the original sin of Adam. Like any valuable thing in life, even forgiveness is costly.

Jesus said that people would recognize us as His disciples by the way we love one another (John 13:35). One huge way love is expressed is in forgiveness. Forgiveness points others to God as the great Reconciler when they see reconciliation through His people.

It's been said that nothing in this world bears the impression of the Son of God so profoundly as forgiveness. The apostle John's implication of forgiveness was clear. He said in John 3:16 (MSG), *"This is how much God loved the world: He gave his Son, his one and only Son. And this is why: so that no one need be destroyed; by believing in him, anyone can have a whole and lasting life.*

God loved (agape) all of mankind so much that He sent His only Son, Jesus. And He did this so that mankind wouldn't be destroyed and spend eternity in hell as a result of the original sin of disobedience by Adam. Anyone who believes (commits their trust) in God's redemptive message through His Son's sacrificial death, burial, and resurrection has been FORGIVEN, and therefore the sin indictment of death and eternal damnation is voided out because of Christ's blood and God's love.

Next to love (the great commandment), *forgiveness* is the Jesus way of navigating with others on life's journey. It isn't optional (Matthew. 6:14-15), but neither is it easy.

Examples of the Jesus Way

Matthew West is a contemporary Christian music artist and author of the popular song, "Forgiveness." He writes of Renee Napier's journey from the darkness of bitterness into the light of forgiveness …

From Renee Napier:

"I never understood why God would ask Abraham to sacrifice Isaac, the son he waited so long to have. I also always hoped He would never require such a sacrifice of me. Once my first child, a son, was born, I really couldn't understand how Abraham just did

105

what God told him to do. The love a parent has for a child is like no other. God also blessed me with three daughters, the last two being identical twins. I love my children with all my heart and could never imagine living without one of them. I now have a mission I did not choose: DUI presentations.

May 11, 2002, twenty-four-year-old drunk driver, Eric, killed one of my twins, Meagan, and one of her friends, Lisa, both girls twenty years old. This was devastating for all three families involved and countless friends who mourned the loss of these precious girls. But this is also a story of forgiveness and healing. My family and Lisa's family chose to forgive Eric. We even appealed to have his twenty-two-year prison sentence reduced to eleven years.

Since March 29, 2004, I have traveled all over the country telling this story to thousands of people, mostly teenagers. I always talk about forgiveness because we have learned how powerful it is for everyone. Eric told me he has his eternal salvation because of Meagan and Lisa. I show him via video in my presentations and will soon have him as an inmate, standing with me, a living, breathing example of the dangers of drunk driving, but also of the power of forgiveness."

In Philip Yancey's book *What's So Amazing About Grace?* he describes forgiveness as an unnatural act. I could not agree more. He writes, "I never find forgiveness easy, and rarely do I find it completely satisfying. Nagging injustices remain, and the wounds still cause pain. I have to approach God again and again, yielding to him the residue of what I thought I had committed to him long ago. I do so because the Gospels make clear the connection: God forgives my debts as I forgive my debtors."

Forgiveness makes little sense as long as we are the ones being asked to forgive. It goes against everything we feel inside when we are the wronged party. And being the flawed humans we are, we do have our limits. However, when we are the ones in need of forgiveness, well, isn't that quite a different story? C.S. Lewis wrote, *"To be a Christian means to forgive the inexcusable, because God has forgiven the inexcusable in you."* Let's always be mindful of our own deep and endless need for forgiveness and grateful for the limitless forgiveness that is extended to us through Christ's sacrifice on the cross. Let's be grateful that He didn't wait for us to make the first move. *"For God demonstrates his great love for us in this; while we were still sinners Christ died for us."* (Romans 5:8) God initiated forgiveness of our sins through every drop of blood that His Son shed, and in doing so released its powerful healing into the lives of all who would be both recipients as well as transporters of that forgiveness.

Seemingly Impossible Forgiveness

After the Second World War, still suffering physical and emotional scars from Nazi brutality, Corrie Ten Boom felt called to preach forgiveness through Europe as people dug out of the war's emotional rubble. She had lost most of her family in concentration camps for helping in the rescue of Jews. She was sure she had overcome her own desire for vengeance against the German SS troops who had dehumanized her and her loved ones in those camps. One occasion took her to Munich. Outside a church after the Sunday service, she found herself looking hard in the face of an old SS guard. He had watched and sneered at frightened women prisoners as they were forced to take delousing showers in front of him. Suddenly for Corrie the memories were there again—the roomful of mocking men, the pain and shame of it all. Now with the war over, the man had come up to Corrie, beaming and bowing politely. "How grateful I am for

[Handwritten annotations in top margin: "unforgiveness, poison we drink, forgive for self, others, God"]

[Handwritten annotation in left margin: "dump out the ailment and the spiritual damage"]

your message," he said. "To think, as you say, that he has washed my sins away." He put out his hand to her. It was too much for Corrie and she kept her hand frozen at her side. Forgiveness comes hard for anyone, and it seemed outrageous to expect it of her at that time, in that situation.

She goes on to tell in her book, *The Hiding Place*, how at that moment angry and vengeful thoughts boiled through her system. She struggled to raise her hand, but she could not. She felt nothing, no emotion of the slightest spark of forgiveness. So she breathed a silent prayer, "Jesus, I cannot forgive him. Give me your forgiveness." And Corrie was touched in that instant by the One who can forgive everyone everything, because He Himself had born the cost of those actions, the cost of forgiveness, on the Cross in His own body. Corrie felt the force of her own forgiveness and the understanding of that forgiveness. In the freedom of being forgiven, she raised her arm and took the hand of the man who had done unforgettable things to her.

Corrie was later to say: "*We never touch the ocean of God's love so much as when we love our enemies. It is a joy to accept forgiveness, but it is almost a greater joy to give forgiveness.*"

[Handwritten: "deep spiritual significance" "means complete, perfect"]

[Handwritten: "Matt 18 70x 7 = 490" "490 = nativity / Bethlehem"]

Amazing Forgiveness

We demonstrate our own experience of God's forgiveness by the way we extend it to others. What could be a greater witness to the truth of the gospel of love and forgiveness than the sight of Elisabeth Elliot (*Through Gates of Splendor*) in Berlin, walking along arm in arm with two Auca Indians who some years before as unbelievers had murdered her husband in the jungles of Ecuador and made her a widow. They were with her then at the Berlin World Congress of Evangelism in 1966. Since they didn't know anything about

[Handwritten left margin: "forgive us + bread go together"]

[Handwritten at bottom: "Forgive us this day our daily" "As we forgive our debtors, debts" "Give us this day our daily bread"]

Need to forgive self first
Need to understand
live by the Holy spirit, God's love/acceptance

Western civilization and had come straight from the jungle, she was teaching them how to use a knife and fork, how to use the toilet, and all the other things necessary for coping with modern ways of living. Forgiveness had healed the pain of Elisabeth Elliot and extracted the anger and resentment that she once felt toward these now Jesus-believing men. NOTHING can do such sobering acts of transformation to the human heart than the power of *forgiveness*.

Jesus put great divine emphasis on the absolute importance of forgiving others who have wronged us. Listen to the famous exchange that Jesus had with Peter.

"Then Peter came up and said to him, "Lord, how often will my brother sin against me, and I forgive him? As many as seven times?" Jesus said to him, "I do not say to you seven times, but seventy times seven." (Matthew 18:21–22)

1490 yrs.

Jesus went on of course to tell the parable of the unforgiving servant. But in this brief exchange, Peter was dead serious about his question. To paraphrase, "Lord, how often does my brother have to hurt me and basically treat me with disdain before I can stop forgiving him? I mean, can seven times be enough?" Peter was probably thinking, at some point there has to be an end game here. But the Jesus way went far beyond anything that Peter could have imagined. "No, Peter, seven times isn't enough. I'm talking infinity here!" Peter wouldn't completely understand the full weight of these words until he held the "Peter, do you love me?" conversation with Jesus in John 21.

490 yrs Jews physical set free from captivity

for complet forgiveness to come thru christs sacrifice

490 yrs - for complet atonement

Bread/wine = communion breaking of christ on the cross

Dan 9
Gabriel - 70 yrs. in Babylon
490 yrs. complet atonement

[handwritten: Moses - turned Water into blood/death. Jesus - turned water into wine/life. Move forward]

We Know We Should but We Don't Know How

Forgiveness isn't optional with God. Yes, admittedly there's pain, anger, and even a sense of injustice about it, but it is the ONLY way to emotionally, relationally, and spiritually move on in life and be free of the anger and resentment that unforgiveness carries. It's the mixture of choosing humility and obedience that produces forgiveness. It's the becoming weak that produces strength. It's in the dying that we gain life and from being humbled that we're made powerful. Forgiveness is a mindset that decides to release rather than hold on to, to be freed rather than to be emotionally and relationally held hostage. It's one of those "It sounds good, but how do you do it?" kind of things. *[handwritten: Why reject being humble? cause, Why me! I didn't cause this]*

Personally I'm convinced that most people, in particular Christians, know they need to forgive, but they just don't know how to forgive. We understand it and accept it "theologically" but struggle with knowing how to apply it practically. For instance, let's take the old saying, "Forgive and forget." Just the term itself doesn't make any sense. That's like saying, "I know you've physically and emotionally abused me for twenty years, but hey, I'm just going to hit the delete button in my brain. All of those painful memories will be completely erased just as soon as I say the magic words, *I forgive you*." You can't just bypass the function of the temporal lobe of your brain, the part of the brain that stores our memory. It's the *hippocampus* part of the brain that retains long-term memory. To somehow think that we can override and wipe clean this vastly complicated central nervous system that God has placed in our cranium with just saying, "I forgive you" is ludicrous, not to mention minimizing God's highly complex and miraculous handiwork. If it were that easy, none of us would have any unpleasant memories from our past. Birds would always

[handwritten left margin: this is not my fault i didn't cause this. Why should i give in? Pride jealous]

[handwritten bottom: bread → forgiveness. breaks bread = breaks body on cross. We can't live physically w/o bread →]

Can't perfect faith but none of us are innocent unless you learn to forgive

pride is still setting in spirit

sing joyfully around us, the sky would constantly be a beautiful blue, there would be no sad experiences, and when we opened our mouths to talk, rainbow-colored Skittles would shoot out!

"I'm innocent. They aren't"

It's important for us to forgive, yes, but it's not good for us to forget. Think about it. When your children were small and one of them touched the hot stove with their hand, did you want them to forget that experience? No, of course you didn't. Why? If they forgot the experience and the pain that it caused, then they would be walking around with charred hands all of the time. I can forgive, but I don't want to forget the imprisoned effect that unforgiveness had on me. I don't want to forget just how debilitating the person who caused me the pain made me live. That person, and the offense connected to the person, tried to define me in terms of the anger, resentment, and bitterness that followed me throughout the years and bled over into other relationships. These are things that you don't want to forget. To forget is not to connect to the pain. It's out of the pain that we find our healing, and we also find out just who we are and who God is in the healing process. No, forgiving is not forgetting. Nor is it excusing. But rather, it's attaching yourself to the reality of the pain that it has caused while at the same time releasing the person who has caused the pain. *It's a decision to release, to let go of your right to continue punishing the other person.* It's asking God to help you, through His love, to release the offender and the offense rather than hold on to them.

How then does someone forgive a person who has hurt them without retaining the anger and resentment after forgiving them? Multiple people have said to me in counseling sessions, "Dr. A, I've done that. I've forgiven them, but I still have great anger toward them. This makes me feel like a failure as a Christian." Along with feeling this way, we experience guilt, shame, condemnation, and a

Man fell on 6th day on fruit on tree — cursed down of thorns etc.

Man stole from garden

Jesus died on tree to remove the curse

can't live spiritually w/o bread of wine = absolutely abundantly living forgiveness

6 stone pots - Man created 6th day on Good Friday 6th day

sense that God just doesn't work for us. Somehow we just can't get it right, can't stack up to what God wants us to do. Therefore it must be us. We're the problem. It certainly can't be God, so we eventually come to the conclusion we're the one who's broken. That's the natural opinion that the enemy wants us to come to so that we can stay *stuck* in our defeatist, self-pitying frame of mind. Jesus gives us, I believe, some insight on this in Matthew 6:14.

> *"For if you forgive other people when they sin against you,*
> *your heavenly Father will also forgive you."*

The word "forgive" here means to *send away*, to *let go*, to *give up a debt*, to not be *hindered* anymore. This is the glorious outcome of forgiveness. We are no longer hindered or obstructed in our lives by the person who wounded us, the person who has been the center of our anger and resentment. Through forgiveness, the offense becomes reduced in our minds and thoughts. It's no longer on the front burner of our psyche so as to affect our walk with Jesus and others. That equals emotional FREEDOM!

The How To

The best model that I personally have ever seen for effective and life-giving forgiveness is twofold.

First, we have to go to the *epicenter*, the cause of the anger and resentment. If I don't go here first, then I'm just addressing symptoms and not the main reason of my anger.

After you've touched "the source" of the pain that has caused you to be triggered by your angry emotions through life and have walked them out in therapy, then I ask the client to write a letter to the person who has wounded them. This is a letter that will not be mailed nor one the abuser will ever see. It's strictly for the purpose of therapy, to touch the pain that's been caused as well as undo the crippling emotions that have been tied to the abused and the abuser.

In his book, *Forgiving Our Parents Forgiving Ourselves*, Dr. David Stoop, when working on his own unforgiveness from childhood trauma, laid out six effective steps of forgiveness. To connect with these steps and viscerally "go there" with the Holy Spirit has proven immensely liberating to many sufferers of unforgiveness, including me.

The Six Steps of Forgiveness
1. Recognize the injury
2. Identify the emotions involved
3. Express your hurt and anger
4. Set boundaries to protect yourself
5. Cancel the debt (forgive)
6. Consider the possibility of reconciliation

> NOTE: Even when implemented, these steps need to be *walked out* to a place of emotional and relational liberation. Rome wasn't built in a day, and neither will the experience of complete forgiveness and freedom over anger and resentment be built in a day. All things of worth take time … forgiveness included. Dr. Stoop went on to say that *"forgiveness is a process that leads us to forgive all those who have hurt us—including ourselves!"* Nothing worth really having comes quick or easy, nor should it.

I have to *recognize* that the offender has emotionally injured me, that the injury is real … it really happened. Then I have to connect with the destructive emotions that I've traveled with. I have to *identify* them, like frustration, depression, impatience, confusion, self-deprecation, etc. I also then have to *express* and release those painful injuries. If I don't get this out, then all of these emotions remain in me, to continue to define just who I am and how I must react to people around me when triggered in life.

To set *boundaries* then becomes a good and healthy thing. Example: less time around the person, leaving his/her presence when you feel you are being triggered, not allowing certain conversations that are upsetting when near this person to go on around you. When it comes to sexual trauma, it is clearly not allowing yourself to be around the person at all.

Now you're ready to *cancel* the debt. Why? You now have more clarity about just why you've been so angry, moody, and agitated throughout the years. You also have a much better understanding of just why you need to forgive this person. They're tied to you in an unhealthy way, and you have to untie them from you. If you don't, then all of the history and the emotional connection tied to that history must then continue to plague you throughout your life, hindering you from God's genuine freedom found in Christ.

You might say, "Well, Fred, I really never get angry. I just kind of process it and move on, so I don't feel I have to address step 3 about expressing the anger." Really? Anger is a multi-headed beast, and it comes in seven forms.

1. Irritation
2. Frustration
3. Grudge
4. Resentment
5. Contempt
6. Hate
7. Rage

When we think of anger, we normally think of the last one, RAGE. However, the other six often play into the way we act out as well. All of them collectively make up how we face and deal with life relationally. If you're thinking that you're not angry because you don't rage, you may want to reconsider.

According to Dr. Stoop, *"Without anger, most forgiveness is superficial. Genuine forgiveness almost always includes anger."* I completely agree with Dr. Stoop.

And then there is considering the possibility of *reconciliation.* This step should be considered when it comes to marital unforgiveness and unforgiveness relating to parents, family, or even friends. However, when it comes to forgiveness relating to sexual abuse, reconciliation is accomplished in the *heart* rather than in person or in any form of reconnecting with the abuser. Most often it isn't wise for sexually abused individuals to be around or even reconnect (in proximity) with their abuser. Forgiveness is an act of obedience that comes from the heart (*soul*, *mind*) and can very well be accomplished in that way.

Time Is a Good Thing

Forgiveness is not natural to our human condition. We don't normally forgive easily. Even when we do forgive, with some it's like having one eye open and one eye closed. I forgive you with the closed eye, but the other eye is open "watching you!" In other words, you have to earn back my trust because you've hurt me. So I'll be watching you with at least one eye until that trust builds up. There are even times when a person feels a sense of unfairness in having to forgive someone.

I believe Jesus understood this in following through with Matthew 18 where Peter is asking, *"How often will my brother sin against me, and I forgive him?"* Jesus realized that this type of agape-driven God mentality wasn't at all natural for Peter or for anyone, in particular in the violent Roman-controlled Middle East at that time. Actually, the lack of that God mentality still exists to this day in many parts of the Middle East. Again, it's a heart thing. Forgiveness comes from the heart, the soul, and the mind. It's the very deepest part of human experience. The feelings of our heart come from the buried caverns of our psyche. Forgiving is a *conscious decision*, a *choice*, an act of obedience. Once we've acted, it is then up to the Holy Spirit to help us walk the act of obedience out. And He does that often in us slowly. When you drive slow, you can see and appreciate much more than if you drive fast. You also have a better chance of not getting into an accident. Slow is good when it comes to forgiveness. You learn through the forgiveness journey and can take your time processing through your act of obedience.

Unforgiveness Can Mess You Up

Through studies, we're finding out more about the negative effects of unforgiveness on a person.

Dr. Carl Thoresen, a professor at Stanford University, and his colleague, Dr. Fred Luskin, explored whether the unresolved anger that affects many people's lives can be alleviated with the help of an age-old Christian concept, forgiveness. After twenty-five years of working with "Type A" personalities (people who are characterized by impatience, being quick to anger, and harboring hostility), Dr. Thoresen ended up seeing for himself over and over the physical and psychological benefits that forgiveness can bring.

Karen Swartz, MD, an associate professor of psychiatry and director of clinical and educational programs at the Johns Hopkins

Mood Disorders Center in Baltimore, Maryland, did a study on the health benefits of forgiveness. Here are a few quotes from Dr. Swartz in reference to her study.

"Withholding forgiveness can put a person in an 'ongoing stress response' that is associated with increased blood pressure, an impaired immune system, anxiety disorders, and depression."

"Reconciling with someone who has injured you, emotionally or otherwise, might not be possible. The goal is for the individual to *not* be dominated by negative thoughts and feelings. It is important to get to a point where you don't define yourself by the betrayal and you move on to healthy relationships."

Go figure, the psychiatric and medical communities are just now finding out what Jesus and His believers have been preaching through the Holy Spirit for over 2000 years now ... forgiveness works!

Forgiveness clearly has emotional, physical, relational, and spiritual benefits attached to it. At the moment of Adam's fall from grace, God had foreknown that forgiveness was the only remedy that could reunite man back to His heart. But how could this be done? Only through sacrifice, only through a means that would not be easy. To be offended and disregarded by someone you loved and who appeared to love you back must have been beyond heart-wrenching. Though Adam and Eve and all of mankind didn't deserve it, His plan for redemptive forgiveness started that day in Genesis 3:7 and led all the way to *"For God so loved the world that He gave His only begotten Son ...."* Only the power of forgiveness provides the needed peace that man requires to be able to effectively walk his days out upon this sin-stained earth. Without it, our hearts become hardened by the same influence that took out Adam. That deceptive and dark voice of the "prince of this world" that says "Injustice doesn't deserve forgiveness." That voice is not the voice of God, and it certainly is not the voice of His Son Jesus.

If it weren't for the power of forgiveness, our collapsed human depravity that has linked us all to Adam would still be crying out for redemption from our sins. It's because of the very act of forgiveness that we have hope today for eternity. When it comes to our freedom from wrongs suffered here on this side of heaven, I believe Dr. Martin Luther King said it best, *"Darkness cannot drive out darkness; only light can do that. Hate cannot drive out hate; only love can do that."* Forgiveness, through an act of loving obedience, is the only key that unlocks this truth.

7

THE JESUS WAY OF LOVE

"If I have the gift of prophecy and can fathom all mysteries and all knowledge, and if I have a faith that can move mountains, but do not have love, I am nothing..."

— 1 Corinthians 13:2

In November of 2006, Ted Haggard, former senior pastor of New Life Church in Colorado Springs, Colorado, and then president of the 30,000,00-member National Association of Evangelicals, resigned from all leadership positions confessing to a personal moral failure. Ted then submitted to church authorities for a two-year period of healing and restoration. Sounds sad, then potentially hopeful, doesn't it? However, there's a backstory of broken promises, untruths, power struggles, and synthetic love that can make for an emotionally tear-jerking movie. Because of all of the scandalous dirt on Ted that has been out there for years, rehashed and dramatized over and over in the media, I'd rather just concentrate on one area here: the absence of genuine Jesus love toward the struggling and broken.

Moral failures are not uncommon in any arena of life, be it religious, political, corporate, or as close as right down the street from you or possibly even within your own home. The weaknesses of man have been with us since Adam and as recent as this morning. In trying to maintain a moral life that is true to the teachings of Jesus and His apostles, we need to understand that there is still the potential for fallibility in all of us as a result of living in these fallen jars of clay. No, not everyone falls into sexual immorality, but all of us fall one way or another. To somehow think that we don't is the ultimate in pride and arrogance.

Back in the fall of 2009, my wife Debbie and I were at my son and daughter-in law's house watching an HBO special by Alexandra Pelosi called *The Trials of Ted Haggard*. Stephen and Keena had suggested that we see it. So one weekend when we were visiting them, we decided to give it a look. It was a documentary about how Ted's career abruptly ended, sending him and his family into a life-changing free fall. His worldwide bombshell scandal not only rocked the ministry, but everyone who knew him, especially his wife Gayle and their five children.

As I watched the documentary, instead of feeling that I'd like to know more about the scandal, I found myself instead thinking, *Who's loving this man and his family back to life?* Where are these people who should be helping and loving them? Who are they? And why does it appear that Ted and his family have been exiled and thrown (metaphorically) into the Egyptian desert? It was so sad to watch this once highly respected, sought out minister now alone and seemingly abandoned by the people (Christian leaders) who should be loving him and his family back to health. Before his fall, Ted would meet with the president of the United States one day, the prime minister of the UK another day, highly profiled Christian leaders the next week, and now he's walking his son's fish tank up a flight of stairs at a cheesy motel where he and his family are spending a few nights. What an unbelievable dichotomy. I just kept thinking, *Where are his advocate leaders and why are they not helping him and his family through this trail of tears?*

I get it…. Because of his actions, he had to step down from his ministry position. I understand that. That makes sense. But where are those from the *household of love*, the Body of Christ, and the healing leaders who are supposed to be "bandaging their wounds" [by] "pouring oil and wine" in them? And also why weren't they staying with them, communicating with them, and taking care of them to a place of healing and restoration?. I know there were some monies given to Ted and his family for counseling, but that's not all that they needed. They needed real flesh and blood, loving, concerned, and caring human beings who would walk with them, keeping up with them and encouraging them on their road to recovery. I mean, isn't that what Jesus taught … and did?

In Jesus' parable of the Good Samaritan, not only did the Samaritan bandage up the poor wounded man on the side of the road, he also, personally, took him to a safe house for recovery and then put the cost of the recovery on his tab. He said, *"And when I return, I will reimburse you for any extra expense you may have."*(Luke 10:35) The guy was coming back! He wasn't going to leave the beat-up man there all by himself. He had plans to return and take further care of him.

Where are the *returners*? Where are those who keep coming back, sticking with you, calling you, dropping in on you, and encouraging you back to emotional and spiritual steadiness? Where are the ones who will weep with you as well as rejoice with you and help protect you until the storm seems less ominous? Restoration is not one-dimensional. It's not just "Here's a few bucks … wish you the best!" For too long many of us in the Body of Christ have suffered from *attachment phobia* when it comes to our brothers and sisters who have fallen into sin. I want to help you, but I really don't want to be attached to you because the stigma and (church) peer pressure just becomes too much. What a blinding of our own feeble self-righteousness! For some outlandish reason, we actually at times think that it couldn't be us on the other side asking and hoping that someone would show us some loving understanding, some grace, and an extended hand of kindness to help us up.

Paul had it right about all of us when he said to the church at Corinth;

"...and we are just as capable of messing it up as they were. Don't be so naive and self-confident. You're not exempt. You could fall flat on your face as easily as anyone else."

1 Corinthians. 10:12 (MSG)

The good news here is that the Haggards' faith in Jesus, even though greatly tested, ended up proving very strong. Their marriage has never been more vibrant, and they're now pastoring again in Colorado Springs, CO. Their children, though shaken up, have stood the test of the storm and remain close and supportive to their mom and dad.

But still, I remember saying out loud while we watched the documentary, *"Wow! This isn't the way we're supposed to treat one another. This isn't love. This isn't Christ's agape."* The Haggards are just one example of so many in the greater Body of Christ who have been disregarded when it comes to showing the true Jesus Way of love.

The Divine and the Human

As much as we would all like to love in the exact way, manner, and spirit that Jesus did, in reality we can't. We'd always like to unconditionally extend forgiveness, compassion, grace and mercy to everyone. But as much as we try, our human condition constantly gets in the way. Yes, it's true Jesus was human, but He was also Divine. There was this mixture of being fully man and fully God. Now that's got to be interesting. *in future sanctification*

Jesus was able to view people in a multifaceted way. He sees us as we *can* be, as a result of His finished work on the cross, even though we are fallen and sinful people. This means that we have the supernatural ability in Christ to be able to change our negative learned behavior life patterns and turn them into opportunities for relational success. What does this look like? For instance, if normally I'm slow to give grace and tolerance to someone, then by looking at my deficiencies and asking the Holy Spirit to help me with them, I can take the first step towards getting better. Always the best first step is ownership (taking responsibility). If I don't see my relational deficiencies and I'm not even willing to be open to see them, then it's going to have to be the other person who does all of the changing... and that never works.

The big difference between Jesus and us is that Jesus IS love and we're not. He was the ultimate expression of the Father's love to all of humanity, God incarnate. *"Whoever does not love does not know God, because God is love."* (1 John 4:8) Christ's very essence is love (agape), and it's impossible for Him to be anything other than what He is. This essence of the Father's love, His Son Jesus, was then transported to earth and He then demonstrated that love through a human form. Acting out of love came natural to Jesus, even when slandered, maligned, ridiculed, and hated. His very words when maliciously treated were so unnatural to the way that we would respond.

"You have heard that it was said, 'Love your neighbor and hate your enemy.' ⁴⁴ But I tell you, love your enemies and pray for those who persecute you…." — Matthew 5:43–44

This is insane! Who practices this kind of craziness … in particular in the Middle East? Yet, this is the Divine leaking out into the human and letting us all know that it's possible to love in such a manner. He realized our natural fallen tendency to do the opposite. He was keenly aware of the angry, revengeful heart of man and the devastation that it was capable of when it came to hate. His way to love was a marker for us to reach, a goal for us to attain, at least to the degree that we struggling mortals can.

All of us have the capacity to love. God placed that emotion in each human being at conception, although sometimes the ability to love gets marred and damaged because of negative or wounding experiences from our childhood or adulthood that make us angry and distant. Jesus was wounded in many ways here on earth, in particular in the last three years of His life. But the Divine part of Him was stronger than the human side, even though they fought against each other. Unlike us, Jesus loved perfectly. He saw the shortcomings and failures of man, but extended compassion, understanding, forgiveness, and grace anyway. But when we experience someone's wrath or them being dishonest or indignant toward us, it's normally "off with their heads!"

You see, that's the difference between Jesus and us, and that's where we need to give ourselves a little slack when it comes to our human failings … however, not too much slack. Yet through all of our struggles, still, Jesus calls us to love as he loves, which says that it's possible.

"A new commandment I give to you, that you love one another: just as I have loved you, you also are to love one another." (John 13:34)

Loving like Jesus loves requires us knowing two things. First, to realize that living the Jesus Way of Life is really nothing shy of impossible. And second, to then come to the clear understanding that with God the Father, *all* things are possible. (Matthew 19:26)

Wanting to show true agape is the longing for His divinity to be shown through our humanity, as flawed as it is. We're the conduit. He's the force of true love shooting through us. When we allow this to happen, His unrestricted agape love not only reaches its intended destination, but it also penetrates into our hearts and changes forever the way we love people. Now that's cool!

The Face of the Adulterous Woman

Though I've already touched on this woman, there's a little something more I'd like to add that I think may be helpful.

In John chapters 7–8, we see that Jesus started out teaching at the Jewish Festival (Feast) of Tabernacles in Jerusalem. He left the city that night to find shelter for the evening, maybe with a friend or just pitching a tent with a few of his disciples. Whatever his arrangements were, he ended up staying and resting around the area of the Mount of Olives. In the big city during the festival, things in some pockets of Jerusalem could get a little crazy at night with drinking, partying, and rowdiness. Jesus decided to leave the city for the night so he could spend some quiet time with the Father and then return early in the morning to finish teaching in the temple. Besides, certain Jewish leaders in Jerusalem wanted to do Jesus harm, and the backdrop of a wild night in the city could have proved dangerous for him.

At sunrise the next morning, Jesus again found himself where he left off the day before, in the temple courts as the main attraction to the most controversial event going on at the festival. To have people come out in droves at the crack of dawn in the middle of a large city to hear you preach is every minister's dream. There were those who were legitimately curious to hear His new and radical teachings on love and forgiveness, and others were there to specifically agitate the crowd and try to discredit what Jesus had to say. They were all there—the poor, the not so poor, the skeptical, the burdened, the hungry, the persecuted, the trouble makers, the lame, the blind, those who kept the law, those who didn't … all of them sheep from the lost house of Israel.

All kinds of things were being said about Jesus while he taught at the temple courts those couple of days. Some were saying that He was "demon-possessed," others said that He was a "prophet," and then there were those who said He was the "Messiah." Never before had anyone seen such a stir at the Jewish festival as when this self-proclaimed carpenter Messiah showed up. It appeared He was the hot topic of everyone's conversation, whether pro or con. And then there were the agitators in the crowd. Many of these rebel rousers were paid off and planted by the Pharisees to repeatedly hit Jesus time and time again with disrespectful and attacking statements meant to discredit Him and cause a ruckus with the crowd so as to hopefully turn them against Him. It was just another day on the job for Jesus. It wasn't as if He hadn't heard this stuff before. Nor would it be the last time He would hear it either.

As the crowd was gathering around Jesus this early morning to hear Him teach, off to the side He saw some teachers of the law and Pharisees bringing a woman with them. They made her stand right in the middle of the group of people who had come to hear Jesus. With a stern, condescending, and self-righteous voice, one of the Pharisees said, "Teacher, this woman was caught in the very act of committing adultery. If you're a real teacher of the law, then you must know that in the Law, Moses commanded us to stone, put to death, a sinful woman like this. Now, you tell us, what do you say that we do?" They loved it! What a moment! It was a picture perfect, Pharisaical snake pit dream question.

We all know what happened and that Jesus hit the hypocrites with the classic return comeback punch, *"You who are without sin cast the first stone."* But what you might not know is that the Law vipers couldn't have stoned this woman to death anyway ... at least *they* didn't have the power to do it. You see, even though Jewish law required that a woman caught in adultery was to be stoned to death, legally the Jews couldn't take that matter into their own hands. And the reason they couldn't was because all Jews at this time were under Roman law, and Roman law superseded Jewish law, or any law for that matter. Roman law at that time was supreme and final. The woman would have to be brought before a Roman judge first and then it may or may not go the Jewish way. More often in cases like this, it didn't. Roman leaders didn't particularly like the Jews and thought even less of their customs.

Jesus (and the Pharisees) clearly knew that only Roman officials had the authority to give out capital punishment. Perhaps even the woman knew as well. More than anything, it was a public display of humiliation toward the woman and a seemingly perfect chance to get Jesus, as a Jew, to speak against the Law of Moses. "Is your allegiance to Moses and the Law, or is it with Rome, Jesus, when it comes to this offense?" If He said Rome, then that does it: He's no Messiah, because the Messiah would never contradict the Law. Neither would He be a good Jew for that matter, because a good Jew would never speak against the Law of Moses, even if they were under another ruler. Then again, Jesus knew that under Roman law he also had no authority to say, "Yes, stone her." Remember, Jesus was a *"give to Caesar what is Caesar's"* guy (Mark. 12:17). He wasn't a subversive zealot like some of the other Jews. Even His apostle, Paul, would later say in Romans 13:1, *"All of you must obey those who rule over you."*

In the middle of all of this drama was the woman who had sinned and was being disgraced and humiliated before everyone. She had made a mistake. Possibly she was a prostitute, and this kind of sad life was the only thing she could do to make some money. She was most likely broken, suffering from a painful past, and maybe even a traumatized or sexually abused childhood. Feeling that she was worthless, had little to give, and had already made a mess of her life anyway, she resorts to being used. Having no conception of what real love even means or looks like, she degrades herself. I wonder what she was thinking while they stood her in public shame? Was she more afraid of being taken to trial or even worse, killed? Or was she overwhelmed by this total stranger, a Jew, and a man at that, coming to her defense, not only fighting for her safety, but turning the tables on her accusers.

And I wonder what she was thinking when it was all over and she was by herself?

Why would this man, a Jew, a teacher of the Law, stand up and defend me knowing what I had done? I don't get it. This doesn't make sense. He should have been over there with them judging and condemning me rather than stooping down writing in the dirt and then standing up and saying, *"you who are without sin cast the first stone."* I can't wrap my head around this ... what? He silenced every one of them. Their jaws dropped, and they didn't know what hit them. It was surreal. But it was His words at the end, those unfamiliar, nonjudgmental words of care and compassion that are still spinning around in my mind that I just can't shake. There weren't many words, but such as they were, I've never heard anyone speak like that. I won't forget those words for as long as I live. He didn't condemn me. Wow! He said I should leave the kind of lifestyle I was living so I would no longer have to live in sin. He didn't condemn nor did He condone, but rather, this man, this teacher of the Jews, showed me *mercy* and gave me a sense of *hope*, and dare I say ... even dignity. He wanted nothing from me but rather gave to me. It feels like He gave me permission to be a better person. Believing that somehow that could be possible .... Could it be? I don't know what real unselfish love and respect feels like, but if it exists, then this is the closest I've ever come to it. Who is this man? I'm hearing on the streets that many are saying He's the Messiah. No way. Really? I mean ... could it be? Is it possible?

Any of our faces could have been placed on the face of the adulterous woman. In some way, each of us have been unfaithful to God through our journey in life. Whether that's been through actual adultery or by way of greed, selfishness, unforgiveness, gossip, sexual addiction/sexual sins, pride, gluttony, damaging anger, self-centeredness, bitterness, dishonesty, judging, and the list goes on and on, the fact is we've all fallen short and do fall short every day of our lives. To use the name "Christian" should be more meaningful and hopeful than just wearing it as a religious name that you've tagged yourself with throughout the years. The Jesus style of love expects and even demands godly change in our lives but offers grace, patience, compassion, and mercy on the road to that change. It's a loving hand extended out to lift us up when we've fallen down rather than a whip to make us obey.

Personally, I'm very sorry to say that throughout my younger years in the ministry I tended to show the whip of legalism more than I extended the loving hand of grace and mercy when it came to showing people what Jesus looked like. Unfortunately, legalism in my early Christian ministry walk seemed to trump grace more often when it came to painting a picture of what a Christian was supposed to say, how they were to act, live, and even think. I got the, "thou shalt and shalt nots" down pretty good, but I didn't get the part very well where it said that Jesus was also ".full of *grace* and *truth*" (John 1:14).

If only I had gotten earlier that beautiful revelation that He is *both* of those simultaneously. He is both grace *and* truth together, and to separate one from the other is to divide the Person and the purpose of who He is and what He has come to do for all of us fallen souls. If we don't get that part, that very important part of the Jesus style of loving, then we've ripped the heart out of the message and the power of the Gospel. It's the extension of His "grace" that makes living in His truth possible in these jars of clay.

British theologian and scholar N.T. Wright said, *"When we learn to read the story of Jesus and see it as the story of the love of God, doing for us what we could not do for ourselves—that insight produces, again and again, a sense of astonished gratitude which is very near the heart of authentic Christian experience."*

This style of loving doesn't come easily. It has to be desired, and it's only made alive as we're willing to make it alive through trial and error. In the end, though, we can do it, because God will love through us as a result of who He is and what He has accomplished in His Son. We don't possess in and of ourselves the ability to move this far in agape love. But if we're willing to empty our pain and our natural tendency toward self-centeredness, then we could very well experience what Wright called "[the] astonishing gratitude" of what makes us believers in the Jesus style of love.

ADDICTIONS, JESUS, AND YOUR BRAIN

"Imagine trying to live without air. Now imagine something worse."

— Amy Reed

One of the largest growing epidemics in our society today is the problem of addictions. And this issue doesn't just exist in secular society either. It's also penetrated within the walls of the church.

Addictions come in numerous forms: overeating, sugar consumption, smoking, spending, and gambling/gaming, just to mention a few. But in this chapter I'd like to concentrate on three very specific addictions that are becoming a pandemic in our society as well as in the church. These three highly lethal addictions are: *drug* abuse, *alcohol* abuse, and *pornography* ... the three-headed monster of individual and relational destruction. These three demons are the equivalent of being the psychological, physiological, and neurological "Ebola" of self-destructive human patterns in our day. Let's take a look at just where these vices come from, the way in which they affect us, and how a person can maintain and even be free from them completely.

Pot's No Big Deal...Right?

The pot debate in our country today seems to be more divisive and politically charged than ever before. But here is a quick data synopsis of hard evidence that's staring us in the face.

According to the National Institute on Drug Abuse (NIH), marijuana is the most commonly used illicit drug (19.8 million past-month users) according to the 2013 National Survey on Drug Use and Health (NSDUH). That year, marijuana was used by 81.0 percent of current illicit drug users (defined as having used a drug at some time in the thirty days before the survey) and was the only drug used by 64.7 percent of them.

Marijuana use is widespread among adolescents and young adults. According to the Monitoring the Future survey—an annual survey of drug use and attitudes among the nation's middle and high school students—most measures of marijuana use by eighth, tenth, and twelfth graders have held steady in the past few years following several years of increase in the previous decade. Teens' perceptions of the risks of marijuana use have steadily declined over the past decade, possibly related to increasing public debate about legalizing or loosening restrictions on marijuana for medicinal and recreational use. In 2014, 11.7 percent of eighth graders reported marijuana use in the past year and 6.5 percent were current users. Among tenth graders, 27.3 percent had used marijuana in the past year and 16.6 percent were current users. Rates of use among twelfth-graders were higher still: 35.1 percent had used marijuana during the year prior to the survey, and 21.2 percent were current users. 5.8 percent said they used marijuana daily or near-daily. Now that's a bunch of pot smoking no matter how you light it!

Here's the hard truth. No matter how it gets into your system, it affects almost every organ in your body and your nervous system and immune system, too. When you smoke pot, your body absorbs THC (Tetrahydrocannabinol) right away. THC is the psychoactive compound in marijuana. If you eat a baked good or another item, it may take much longer for your body to absorb THC because it has to break down in your stomach before it enters your bloodstream). However, when you smoke pot, you may notice changes in your body right away. The effects usually stop after 3 or 4 hours.

It's common knowledge in the field of science and medicine that smoking pot can increase your heart rate by as much as two times faster for up to 3 hours. That's why some people have a heart attack right after they use marijuana. It can increase bleeding, lower blood pressure, and affect your blood sugar, too.

Marijuana and the Brain

After you inhale marijuana smoke, its chemicals zip throughout the body. THC is a very potent chemical compared to other psychoactive drugs. Once in your bloodstream, THC typically reaches the brain seconds after it's inhaled and begins to go to work.

Marijuana users often describe the experience of smoking the drug as initially relaxing and mellow, creating a feeling of haziness and light-headedness (although those feelings may differ depending on the particular strain). The user's eyes may dilate, causing colors to appear more intense, and other senses may be enhanced. Later, the user may have feelings of paranoia and panic. The interaction of the THC with the brain is what causes these feelings. To understand how marijuana affects the brain, you need to know about the parts of the brain that are affected by THC.

Your brain has groups of cannabinoid receptors concentrated in several different places. The cannabinoid receptors are part of the endocannabinoid system which is involved in a variety of physiological processes including appetite, pain sensation, mood, and memory. These cannabinoid receptors can affect the following mental and physical activities:

- Short/long term memory
- Coordination
- Learning
- Problem-solving
- Attention/concentration

When the THC binds with the cannabinoid receptors inside the hippocampus part of the brain, it affects coordination, which the cerebellum part of the brain controls. The basal ganglia part of the brain then directs unconscious muscle movements, which is another reason why motor coordination is impaired when under the influence of marijuana.

And to be honest, yes, before I came to Jesus, unlike Bill Clinton (sure, Bill) I did inhale as a teenager... and yes, there is a hallucinogenic factor to marijuana. If anyone tells you otherwise (anyone who has actually smoked it), then they're lying to you. And yes, without question, if there is a genetic propensity in a person's family of origin toward addictions, then absolutely, marijuana can definitely be a "gateway" drug to much more dangerous drugs.

There are four main categories of drugs: <u>stimulants</u>, <u>hallucinogens</u>, <u>opiates,</u> and <u>depressants</u>. Drugs are classified according to their common effects and actions on the mind and body. Marijuana is difficult to precisely categorize because it actually shows signs of all four. It raises your heart rate (stimulant). As for hallucinogen, it can change the way your mind perceives things. Most medical and psychological professionals today classify it as a mild hallucinogen. There is a factor that makes people want to continually use it over and over (opiate). And it generally slows down movement and mood (depressant).

Slowly but surely I'm counseling Christian parishioners and even some pastors who are reverting back to smoking marijuana to "relax their minds" as one pastor told me. But in actuality, it's more of an escapism from the anxiety and sometimes pain of everyday life. I also find people self-medicating on pot because of the need to escape from the sorrow of painful family experiences either in their marriage, with their children, or from their past. That's what marijuana does, it numbs and distorts reality for a person who is wanting to escape from the barrage of life's painful blasts, in particular when they smoke pot into their adulthood.

Heartbroken Christian Parents of Drug Addicts

There are no words that can describe the heartbreak, pain, and emotional trauma that a parent of a drug-addicted child goes through. You may be thinking, "Why are you talking about such a topic in a Christian oriented book?" The tormenting evil of drug addiction is not just limited to the stereo typical homeless person on the street of your intercity. It's also woven within the church and can be as close as your own front door.

There are few things that are more traumatic for parents than to watch their child fall victim to the highly demoralizing effects of drug addiction. For the Christian parent, certain questions emerge. Questions like: our child grew up in the church, went to Christian school, participated in the church youth group, went to Christian camps, and grew up in a stable home—how could this have happened? We've always shared with them about the dangers of alcohol abuse and drugs and how they can lead to a disastrous life. Where did we go wrong?

Most likely you didn't do anything wrong. Parents of a drug addict child need to hear this because always in the forefront of your mind is the notion that it was something that you did or did not do that contributed to their addiction. What could I have done differently, what more could I have said, what "t" did I not cross or what "i" did I not dot that helped lead to my child's addiction? For those parents, I would say this: most likely it's nothing that you did or didn't do. Sometimes bad genetics just don't work in your favor. It's an *Adam* thing. Remember when Adam fell, he fell hard and the generational ripple-down affect has been enormously devastating to humanity ever since.

I'm putting this chapter on drug addiction in my book because there are many parents, both believers and unbelievers, who become the silent sufferers when it comes to having a drug addict child in your nuclear family. The emotionally painful struggle is not just for the addict. It's for the family of the addict as well, in particular the parents.

Dr. Nora D. Volkow, M.D. who is the director of the National Institute on Drug Abuse, says, "For much of the past century, scientists studying drug abuse labored in the shadows of powerful myths and misconceptions about the nature of addiction. When scientists began to study addictive behavior in the 1930s, people addicted to drugs were thought to be morally flawed and lacking in willpower.

Those views shaped society's responses to drug abuse, treating it as a moral failing rather than a health problem, which led to an emphasis on punishment rather than prevention and treatment. Today, thanks to science, our views and our responses to addiction and other substance use disorders have changed dramatically. Groundbreaking discoveries about the brain have revolutionized our understanding of compulsive drug use, enabling us to respond effectively to the problem."

Our Genetic Pinball Machine

If you look into your genetic family pool on both sides of your parents and see any form of addiction (alcohol, drugs, tobacco, eating, gambling, spending, etc.), then this may show up in your children as well. It didn't show up because of something you did or did not do for your child. It showed up because the genetic pinball machine just bounced around until it hit your child. Again, it's a Fall of Man thing. Adam really did screw us all up! Now in no way does this excuse the drug addict from being responsible to work on his/her addiction, but it does at least give an answer to the *cause* of their struggle.

In some people, when they mess with alcohol, drugs, gambling, or even sex, it can unleash such a firestorm of hellish behavior that it can literally destroy them.

The struggle of the family addict is twofold—theirs and yours. God's grace and love is found with both. For the parent, it becomes a journey to get well and tear through the web that has woven both the addict and the parent[s] together in an endless and maddening codependent cycle. You want to help them get better so you take care of them and their needs, hoping that somehow they'll "get it," but they never do. They, on the other hand, because of their addiction, continue to extract endless amounts of money from you while lying, manipulating, and conniving their way in and out of your life. The painful emotional and psychological toll that it can take on a family of an opiate addict can be catastrophic. Because of the addict's neurological and physical addiction to the drug, they've lost their capacity to feel empathy or think logically. The drug has them. They no longer control it, but it now controls them...which means they can't be without it. The opioid has taken them over, and they're now a shell of the person they were before being introduced to its demonic affects. Guilt, shame, depression, self-condemnation, loneliness, despair, hopelessness, fear, worthlessness, demoralization, tortured—these are all words that opioid addicts have described themselves as feeling. Depressed, angry, bitter, frustrated, infuriated, compassionate, anxious, confused, lonely, desperate, weary—these are all words that parents of opioid addicts have described themselves as feeling.

In the end, addiction is a family disease. One person may use, but the whole family suffers. Because of this, both addict and codependent parent[s] have to seek help. Neither can help the other, they can only, by the grace of God, help themselves. Movie actor Robert Downey Jr., no stranger to the demoralizing effects of drugs, said, *"Remember, just because you hit rock bottom doesn't mean you have to stay there."*

For the ***addict***, there are three things they need to do to maintain sobriety.

First:

Come to the place where you can say that you're completely powerless over your addiction.

Second:

Enter into an *Ambulatory Detoxification Program* that is an outpatient model for individuals requiring detoxification from drugs or alcohol, with many of the benefits of inpatient detoxification but in a less-restrictive, cost-effective environment.

Third:

Get (and STAY) in a 12 Step program that will be your lifeline to continued recovery.

For the *parent* to break the *codependent* roller coaster, they would need to do two things.

First:

Join an *Al-Anon/Nar-Anon* support group. Al-Anon/Nar-Anon are independent fellowships with the stated purpose of helping relatives and friends of alcoholics and/or drug addicts. It's a fantastic 12 Step group that will be an enormous source of help and support to you in the struggle with your addict.

Second:

Seek out counseling therapy with a licensed professional (Christian) counselor who will help navigate you through the pain and grief of your addict child. You must also build boundaries and create self-care mechanisms to help you maintain emotional strength and spiritual/mental stability on your road to recovery. You must break the nonstop codependent cycle of providing finances to your addicted child. In the end, 99 percent of your money given supports their drug habit and "nothing" that you do in trying to help them is appreciated by them at all. Drug addiction is a nightmare for the addict, and codependency is a nightmare for the parent[s].

Loving but Not Excusing

It is so easy to become angry and distance yourself from the addict. This is a normal reaction. Loving is tough to do when it comes to your addict. But nonetheless, Jesus has called us to do it, even though at times it's so terribly difficult to give out love. But we need to know that the addict didn't "order up" this horrific disease. Though it would appear that they came to it, in reality it came to them (genetics). Again, this isn't at all an excuse to not deal with the addiction and get well, but it is looking at the pathology of the cause. Addicts don't choose to be addicted. What they're actually doing is denying the pain that is fueling the addiction. This is the case with all addictions. That's the reason for the importance of ongoing counseling therapy and a 12 Step program. It helps them to uncover the pain through the power and leading of the Holy Spirit so that God can remove it from their lives. With a motivated attitude and the grace of God, it is without question possible for them to feel free from their guilt, shame, and addictive prison.

Rather than put her entire story in this book, I'd encourage you to read Shannon Palmer's article called *How the World Sees a Drug Addict*. It's an excellent read on what an opiate addict really experiences through the eyes of someone who's lived it. http://henryharbor.com/how-the-world-sees-a-drug-addict/

Christians and Alcohol Use

Now here's a *hot* topic that's on the front burner of the Evangelical stove. Let's take a look at both sides of the subject.

Kevin P. Emmert in his November 18, 2013 article in *Christianity Today* wrote about how some seminaries and Bible colleges are dropping the bans on drinking as they see alcohol as no longer being morally wrong.

In August 2013, *Moody Bible Institute* lifted its alcohol and tobacco ban for its 600 full-time employees, following recent similar moves by Wheaton College, Huntington University, and Asbury Seminary.

Moody spokesperson Brian Regnerus said the change "came out of a desire in Moody's leadership to reflect a high-trust environment that emphasizes values, not rules," and to "require no more and no less than what God's Word requires."

In a *Lifeway Research, 2007* survey of evangelicals and alcohol, the following information was gathered from their study.

"It's not a sin to drink alcohol."
Protestant pastors, 65%
Protestant Laity, 60%

"I drink alcohol."
Protestant pastors, 22%
Protestant Laity, 39%

Peter Green, whose PhD research at Wheaton focuses on the theological significance of wine and vineyard themes in Scripture, says the Bible presents alcoholic drinks as an indicator and facilitator of human and divine relationships.

"The Old Testament is unambiguous that wine and other alcoholic beverages are a blessing, and their absence is considered a curse," said Green. He acknowledges the Bible forbids drunkenness and that some people should avoid alcohol due to addiction or family history, but he believes that most Christians should imbibe, not abstain.

Christians have always been concerned about drunkenness, but it wasn't until the Protestant social reform movement of the 1800s that temperance was equated with complete abstinence.

"It's an 'American oddity,' said Jennifer Woodruff Tait, managing editor of *Christian History* magazine. "It's not that groups of people throughout history didn't practice complete abstinence. The Nazarites in the Bible didn't drink alcohol. But in the nineteenth century, a whole segment of the church said it's not just an ascetic practice that some people might choose; they said this is for everybody—all Christians must stop drinking or they're not Christians."

That climate has changed, said Larry Eskridge, associate director of the Institute for the Study of American Evangelicals. While not a teetotaler himself, Eskridge said he's fond of the view that has dominated the evangelical landscape. "The underlying sensibility is taking care of your neighbor, taking care of your family, trying to be a good role model, and not being a stumbling block," he said. "Abstinence might easily be the way to go for a lot of people."

And Free Will Baptist Family Ministries in Greeneville, Tennessee, recently cancelled an event featuring "Duck Dynasty" star Willie Robertson because the reality TV family has gone into the wine business. The Robertson family announced at the beginning of November that they reached a deal with Trinchero Family Estates to release Duck Commander Wines. The Greeneville ministry said Robertson's appearance would send a mixed message to the people who go through the organization's drug and alcohol program. "Our message must be consistent. The lives of those children may well hang in the balance," said Derek Bell, director of development for Family Ministries. "We certainly apologize to the people who have already purchased tickets, and pray they understand our position."

To Drink or Not to Drink

As you can see, there are clearly opposing opinions on the subject. But one thing is for certain: if there is a clear history of alcoholism in your family of origin, that's a good indicator for you to not abuse alcohol or for that matter even drink alcohol at all. Why? You might be releasing the genetic "addictive gene" that has been dormant in you so far, and to begin to drink may very well mean "the beast" gets out! Also, consuming alcohol may make matters more difficult for people suffering from mental health conditions like anxiety, depression, bipolar and impulse control disorders. Even having a couple of drinks a day carries consequences that affect brain and body functioning, leaving a negative impact on mental wellbeing. Sometimes, people feeling high amounts of stress, pain, anxiety, and impulse look to alcohol to find short-term relief without realizing that using substances can limit the progress toward reaching long-term emotional stability. Alcohol may cause moodiness, lower inhibitions, upset the cycle of restorative sleep, increase the symptoms of depression, and interfere with prescribed medication. For some, drinking alcohol may become a dangerous coping mechanism, one that can ultimately lead to addiction.

How about Christians drinking in front of other Christians who don't drink alcohol? There are numerous theological opinions and papers written on this subject, but while I'm at it, why not just one more?

The Bible says that *"Wine produces mockers; alcohol leads to brawls. Those led astray by drink cannot be wise."* (Proverbs 20:1, NLT) The Bible also says, *"What sorrow awaits you who make your neighbors drunk! You force your cup on them so you can gloat over their shameful nakedness."* (Habakkuk 2:15, NLT). Yet the Bible does not say that drinking a glass of wine or a beer, or a cocktail with dinner, is a sin. Drunkenness is a sin, forbidden by the Bible, but a drink or two does not appear to be wrong.

But even though the Bible doesn't forbid drinking an alcoholic beverage, still we should not have the mentality that arrogantly says, "I can drink alcoholic beverages wherever I'm at and whoever I'm with because the Bible doesn't say I can't." Well, first, the Bible does say you shouldn't do that.

The apostle Paul teaches us in Romans 14:21–22: *"It is better not to eat meat or drink wine or do anything else if it might cause another believer to stumble. You may believe there's nothing wrong with what you are doing, but keep it between yourself and God."* This isn't exactly a vague comment here by Paul. He's clearly saying that if you have a liberty (like drinking a glass of wine or having a beer), then that's one thing. But if you have that liberty, don't do it "in the face" of another believer who does not have that liberty. Why? It's flat out insensitive and wrong, that's why! Nor is it showing agape love to your brother or sister in the Lord. If you're open to think about it, in the end it's really just an act of arrogant selfishness rather than being sensitive and considerate. Some things just aren't difficult to get...unless you're just a difficult person.

Sex Addiction Comes to Church

It's estimated that half of Christian men have a problem with pornography. Porn is reported to be a 97 billion dollar industry worldwide, 14 billion in the US alone. Pornography generates more money on an annual basis than most sports, television, or other entertainment industries. For example, in the US alone the porn industry generates more annual revenue than ABC, CBS, NBC, FOX,

CNN and MSNBC combined. It also generates more annual revenue than the NFL, MLB, NBA, GM, Ford, and Chrysler combined. It's a massive industry! Unfortunately, the pornography industry views most of the population as their demographic and can target their efforts to everyone with an Internet connection.

According to *Covenant Eyes*, a respected Christian internet accountability and filtering company out of Owosso, Michigan, 64 percent of Christian men and 15 percent of Christian women say they watch porn at least once a month. Patrick Means, author of *Men's Secret Wars*, reveals that 63 percent of pastors surveyed confirm that they are struggling with sexual addiction or sexual compulsion including, but not limited to, the use of pornography, compulsive masturbation, or other secret sexual activity. Nearly 20 percent of the calls received on Focus on the Family's Pastoral Care Line are for help with issues such as pornography and compulsive sexual behavior. And of the 1,351 pastors that Rick Warren's website, Pastors.com, surveyed on porn use, 54 percent said they had viewed internet pornography within the last year and 30 percent of those had visited within the last thirty days.

As much as we would like to think that the walls of the church have been able to successfully insolate pornography from entering in, the fact is it hasn't. And not only has it not kept pornography out, but the grim statistics are also unfortunately climbing. The sole purpose for the porn industry is to have its followers become *addicted* to its product. Why? Sexual addiction, like drugs, is enormously lucrative. They could care less about the relational/moral destructive aspects of its product. All they care about is the money!

Marriage, Porn, and Intimacy

Pornography is unbelievably destructive in any relationship, but particularly in a marriage relationship. Why? The reason is because marriage is the intimate union and equal partnership of a man and a woman. It comes to us from the heart of God who created male and female in His image so that they might become one body together in holy covenant. Marriage is both a natural institution and a sacred union because it's rooted in the divine plan of creation.

"He created them male and female and blessed them. And he named them "Mankind" when they were created." — Genesis. 5:2 (NIV)

Marriage is about *love* (agape), *relationship*, and *intimacy*, the three ways in which we were created to interact with God. On our end, it's not always pretty or perfect in a committed marital relationship throughout the years, but the template that God gave us is just like Alcoholics Anonymous: "It works if you work it."

When pornography enters into God's designed marital covenant, emotional, neurological, and physiological chaos ensues. A fury of chemicals (oxytocin, prolactin, endorphins, testosterone, serotonin, and adrenaline) begins to explode in a male during sexual intercourse. These chemicals have been strategically placed there by God for the purpose not only of sexual stimulation, but also for intimately, emotionally, and spiritually connecting within the confines of a God-designed covenant. Pornography deceives and confuses the mind and body, and makes it attach to a noncovenant image, thus releasing chemicals that connect with an image other than its God-designed focus. This is greatly compounded when the *wife of your youth* has borne your children and may not be quite up to snuff to the imagery of the porn beauties that you're watching.

In her article entitled "The Impact of Pornography on Marital Sex," Juli Stattery says,

"Not only does porn present a higher level of sexual excitement than married sex, it also allows a man to have sex on his terms. Porn is always available, never too busy, and always inviting. It doesn't criticize, doesn't require foreplay or patience, isn't dependent on 'feeling close,' and never has a headache. When a guy is engaged in this type of sexual outlet, his sexuality becomes centered on his immediate needs and demands. The prospect of working through the messy issues of marital intimacy is pretty unattractive."

And there lies the core, or should I say the cause of the problem ... *intimacy*.

Those who struggle with sexual addiction don't enter into sex purely to escape the pressures of everyday life. They use sex as a shallow, fantasy-based substitute for *genuine*, legitimate intimacy. A lack of *genuine* intimacy with addicts often, though not always, comes from some form of trauma as a child. That could be sexual trauma or rejection / abandonment trauma from a parent, normally same-sex parent. Most sex addicts have no idea of how to achieve genuine intimacy, so they act out intimacy through a connection with sex (pornography / affairs) rather than relationship. They form no attachment to their sexual imagery or partners.

The Addiction Cycle

There's a common addiction cycle (ritual) that happens when acting out sexually as a result of some form of childhood trauma.

First, there's a longing for intimacy and closeness that wasn't met in childhood.

Second, that intimacy void then acts out sexually in some form.

<u>Third</u>, guilt, shame, and condemnation enter in making the addict feel less than and worthless … distant from God.

<u>Forth</u>, after some time and sobriety, the addict gradually works himself/herself back to a place where he/she doesn't feel so distant from God. This is after many prayers and promises to not return again to their sin of sexually acting out.

<u>Fifth</u>, a return to sexually acting out and the cycle (ritual) begins all over again.

This cycle actually happens in any form of addiction, whether that is sex, drugs, food, gambling, spending, etc. In the end, it all comes from a wound (trauma) in some form or another and more likely a childhood trauma. A Christian recovery center with professional therapists who specialize in sexual addiction is the absolute best place to go to uncover the *cause* of the reason that a person acts out in unhealthy sexual behavior.

Marriage Conflict and Distance

As a crisis marriage therapist, I've found that when there is a deep divide in the marital relationship, then distance, lack of communication, feeling misunderstood, unappreciated, a lack of affection, and even resentment is often present when sexually acting out. This clearly isn't the case with all couples, but where there has been the presence of childhood abuse or even parental abandonment, it does tend to be more prevalent. Again, the reason is because the persons who are acting out sexually are looking (longing) for legitimate and genuine intimacy … the thing that has evaded them throughout their life. As deeply important as those two needs are, what we must understand is that *ultimately* genuine intimacy can only be made life-giving through the person of Jesus Christ. This is true whether there has been childhood trauma in your life or not. Ultimately, true and life-giving closeness, affection, understanding, love, and relationship can only be found and expressed between the Creator and His human creation. It's there that we both find our emotional peace and our true designated identity. Look at what Jesus said about intimate relationships.

"This is my command: Love one another the way I loved you. This is the very best way to love. Put your life on the line for your friends. You are my friends when you do the things I command you. I'm no longer calling you servants because servants don't understand what their master is thinking and planning. No, I've named you friends because I've let you in on everything I've heard from the Father." (John 15:15, MSG) Jesus confine everything to disple

Andrew Murray (1828–1917), the great Dutch Reformed writer, disple teacher, and Christian pastor, said this of true intimacy with Christ:

"'The highest proof of true friendship, and one great source of its blessedness, is the intimacy that holds nothing back, and admits the friend to share our inmost secrets. The servant knoweth not what his Lord doeth,' he has to obey without being consulted or admitted into the secret of all his master's plans. 'But, I have called you friends, for all things I heard from My Father I have made known unto you.' Christ's friends share with Him in all the secrets the Father has entrusted to Him."

Genuine intimacy is the friendship and closeness that "holds nothing back." Not care, value, comfort, respect, compassion, or intimate feeling. That could be either sensual, between a man and a woman, or safe parental closeness that is designed to protect, love, and nurture. When the latter hasn't been met in childhood, then a true understanding of genuine intimacy is nothing but a ghost. You've heard of it but have never seen it. The only thing left then is whatever conception of intimacy your mind can come up with or what your experience was in an environment that was supposed to show legitimate intimacy but didn't. So what happens? You go looking for it, that's what happens. And if the propensity of the person leans toward sexually acting out, then from that experience grows a selfish synthetic form of intimacy. Not a "blessedness" intimacy that Murray talks about, but instead a hollow, dark, and sexually confusing counterfeit form of intimacy that leaves a person guilt ridden, living in shame, and fighting his two worlds between God and the tormenter. And when this psychological/spiritual battle is brought into an already struggling marriage or into the marital bedroom, you can see just how potentially devastating the relationship can end up being.

Where there is the lack of *genuine* intimacy, there is the presence of profound self-centeredness and self-pleasure…a drive to avoid the true pain and seek immediate gratification. The sex addict uses pornography, female/male sexual encounters, fantasy sex, voyeurism, sadomasochistic sex, exhibitionistic sex etc., as a substitute for real genuine human intimacy and relationship.

The church has a lot to catch up on when it comes to addictions.

Addicts come in all shapes and sizes. Some are presidents of companies, public officials, lawyers, plumbers, religious leaders, doctors, and ditch diggers alike. They can be your pastor, elders, deacons, and even Sunday school teachers. Others are your stereotypical street bums, brown bagging it or sleeping on a park bench with filthy, tattered clothes on, reeking of alcohol, tobacco, and body stench. They are our sons, daughters, husbands, fathers, wives, and all in between. But if you could open up their soul and look into any of these struggling addicts, yes, possibly even you or me, you would see the same thing: guilt, sorrow, self-condemnation, shame, regret, and a sense of being terribly alone. Addiction and our flawed human condition all live in the same family, and the ice is very thin between all of us when differentiating sin.

The bad news is if the addict chooses to stay isolated and not go to the places of pain where the true cause of their acting out lives, then they are destined to continue living in their personal hell … something the enemy would love nothing more. But the good news is if they do choose to go to those places through professional counseling, then the sky is the limit when it comes to freedom from their addiction and self-deprecation.

Amelia Earhart said, *"The most difficult thing is the decision to act. The rest is merely tenacity. The fears are paper tigers. You can do anything you decide to do. You can act to change and control your life and the procedure. The process is its own reward."*

Truer words were never spoken when it comes to a person chained to an addiction. Help is available. There just needs to be the first decision to act, and the process is its own reward. Your life doesn't get better by chance; it gets better by change.

It's Still About His Love

Whether it's sex, drug, alcohol, overeating, smoking, gambling, or shopping addictions, the principle of (agape) love should still be at the center of our lives as we navigate through these complications. If we as believers in Christ are to see a God change in all fallen men and women, then we need to first look at our own depravity before pointing the finger at another's. It's our self-centered, at times arrogant, fallen human condition that often doesn't allow us to love first when dealing with such broken and struggling people.

Peter told us, *"Most important of all, continue to show deep love for each other, for love covers a multitude of sins."* (1 Peter 4:8, NLT)

Notice that "deep love" doesn't *excuse* sin, but rather covers it as a damp blanket putting out a fire. Oh, if we could only learn this, what awesome good could we accomplish for Christ in our deeply divided nation?

Paul, a guy who knew a few things about sharing the transforming power of Jesus, laid out a great template for loving people to a place of life change. Building on the words of Jesus, Paul tells us in 1 Cor. 13:4–8: "Love (agape) is patient, kind, not jealous or boastful, not proud or rude, doesn't demand its own way, isn't irritable, keeps no record of being wronged, doesn't rejoice about injustice but rejoices whenever the truth wins out. Love never gives up, or loses faith. Love is always hopeful and endures through every circumstance. Love will last forever."

Jesus loved in such a way that made people feel they were introduced to love for the first time. It made the Samaritan woman say, *"He told me everything I ever did."* With Peter, it compelled him to say *"[You're] the Messiah, the Son of the living God."* And it compelled the inquisitive Pharisee Nicodemus to come and seek out "Jesus at night" to listen to His amazing explanation of how a grown person can be "born again."

Brennan Manning said, *"How glorious the splendor of a human heart that trusts that it is loved!"* That's really the answer for both the addict as well as the person in relationship with the addict. If truly "love never fails," then it's healing and compassionate power extends to the believer as well as the unbeliever. Through the struggle of any form of addiction, ultimately it's the power of His love, the true experience of legitimate *intimacy* with the living God, that always provides lasting fulfillment and hope.

9

THE PIOUS HAND OF LEGALISM

"To be risen with Christ means not only that one has a choice and that one may live by a higher law—the law of grace and love—but that one must do so. The first obligation of the Christian is to maintain their freedom from all superstitions, all blind taboos and religious formalities, indeed from all empty forms of legalism."

— Thomas Merton

Legalism within Christian theology, in its simplest terms is, placing the Law (Old Testament) above the Gospel (New Testament). It's an establishment of requirements (dos and don'ts) that has to be lived out by a person in order to stay within the protection of the salvation that's been given to us through Jesus Christ.

Within Christianity, and specifically within Evangelical Christianity today, legalism has and can be the excessive overemphasis of the Law (Ten Commandments) and other aspects of the law in a person's life. Christian legalists set certain rules and regulations to live by for themselves as well as others in order to achieve both spiritual growth and (continued) salvation.

Legalism in Christianity can be morphed in different ways. There is the person who has to keep the Law as well as all that is taught in the New Testament and live by it in every way everyday so they won't lose their salvation. And then there is the person who judges *others* for not keeping the Law in their specific prerequisite checklist way so as to prove their salvation in order to receive God's "free gift" of grace. To a degree, these people are one and the same. Some of the ways they may feel a person must live in order to maintain their salvation is to not drink alcohol, not go to movies, not use tobacco, dress a certain way, observe and not observe certain holidays, not associating with people who do not share their Biblical views and standards, etc. Christian legalists may tend to express a lack of joy, finding it difficult to appreciate the grace of God through times of temptation and become performance-oriented in order to receive God's love. They can have a critical or even unloving attitude toward those who don't agree with their religious dogma, obsessing over their subscripted standards of behavior, etc.

Legalists have been around way before Christ, and since the Calvinism (vs) Arminianism theological debate and ,there's no doubt that they'll stay around until Jesus comes back. In the meantime, how do we handle both the Biblical command to live a life of righteousness (dos and don'ts) while at the same time living within the grace that has been paid for us through the redemption we have in the Messiah? (Romans 3:21–26) Also, how do we deal with the incongruity of the legalists who quote one way to live while they themselves are falling short of their own words?

Before we look at how to navigate our faith around the heavy hand of pious legalists, let's first take a look at the connection between Jesus and *grace* and in layman's terms just what that means for each of us.

God, Jesus, Grace, and Us

First and foremost, we need to know that grace is not at all dependent on anything that we can do to earn it. It's first free and second it's a gift. You don't *earn* a gift from someone who just wants to give you one, and you don't earn FREE. It's that simple. It's a free gift that God gave us through Christ's death on the cross.

"For by grace you have been saved through faith; and that not of yourselves, it is the gift of God; not as a result of works, so that no one may boast." (Ephesians 2:8–9)

This means that the grace granted to all of mankind for all time is entirely up to God's sovereign (supreme) will and is distributed to each and every one of us as His wisdom and endless loving kindness dictates. The apostle Paul tells us that God's grace is a gift to us, totally undeserved and unearned. God gives it purely because it was His purpose to grant it to all of humanity through His Son, Jesus Christ.

"For God saved us and called us to live a holy life. He did this, not because we deserved it, but because that was his plan from before the beginning of time–to show us his grace through Christ Jesus." — 2 Timothy 1:9 (NLT)

Second, we need to understand that there is no way that grace would even be possible if it weren't for the death, burial, and resurrection of Jesus Christ, the Messiah.

"We all live off his generous bounty, gift after gift after gift. We got the basics (The Law) from Moses, and then this exuberant giving and receiving, This endless knowing and understanding (Grace)— all this came through Jesus, the Messiah." -John 1:17 (MSG)

Before Jesus was born, God had a plan for reconciling (restoring) the Jews to Himself as a result of their many years of obedience to His Law... the Law He gave to Moses sometimes called the Torah or (Pentateuch) of Moses. The word *Pentateuch* is a Greek expression which is not in the Bible but means "five books." This is the name that Christian scholars often refer to when describing the Law.

Genesis	Beginnings
Exodus	Redemption
Leviticus	Holiness
Numbers	Wandering
Deuteronomy	Review

If the Jews could have been *totally* and completely obedient in every way to these five books, then reconciliation with God would have occurred and consequently there would have been no need for a Messiah. However, their sinful human condition prohibited them from being able to accomplish this. In other words, it was impossible. Why? The Law only pointed to our need for a Savior. It was a shadow of the coming Messiah but couldn't at all stack up to Him or what He was going to accomplish for us.

"The old system under the law of Moses was only a shadow, a dim preview of the good things to come, not the good things themselves. The sacrifices under that system were repeated again and again, year after year, but they were never able to provide perfect cleansing for those who came to worship." — Hebrews 10:1 (NLT)

When Christ died on the cross for us, He paid the price for all of mankind's sin, then and until the end of time. As a result, Jesus through His death set us free from that debt (pay back for our sins) to God. Jesus paid it, we didn't. Jesus was God's gift to us, God's *grace* to us so that we now and forever more don't have to pay that debt by trying to keep the Law in order to be right with God and to have Him accept us. We're no longer slaves to the Law, but free to live righteous before God as a result of the finished work of Messiah through His death on the cross.

"Now you are free from your slavery to sin, and you have become slaves to righteous living."

— Romans 6:18 (NLT)

Simply put, the redemption that Jesus provided (clearing the sin debt) equaled a better way than the Law could have ever possibly given us. The Law was impotent for eternal effectiveness and life, while Jesus was filled with eternal effectiveness and endlessly life.

Because our Jesus took the punishment and torture that we deserved as a result of Adam's fall in the garden (SIN), we can now through *grace* have the favoritism and approval of God that we in no way could have earned or even deserved. We owe God nothing nor do we have to earn His favor. It was ALL paid for by His Son, our Savior, Jesus. Wow, that's some AWESOME love!! We are always favored

"How? you ask. In Christ. God put the wrong on him who never did anything wrong, so we could be [made] right with God." — 2 Corinthians 5:21 (MSG)

We are part of God's family

Brennan Manning spoke of love and grace when he said your sin does not

"My trust in God flows out of the experience of his loving me, day in and day out, whether the day is stormy or fair, whether I'm sick or in good health, whether I'm in a state of grace or disgrace. He comes to me where I live and loves me as I am." ostracize you

"Just as I am" from the family God takes me of God.

Jesus ≠ legalism

Jesus and Legalism

bipolar

Jesus was the complete antithesis of what the law keepers were. He replaced legalism with the greater principle of love, and in doing that he crushed the law as it was understood in his day.

The Scribes and Pharisees were well known for their meticulous observation of the commandments found in the Old Testament, even down to the minute details. The legalists were religious leaders who considered themselves very righteous and pious before God because of their disciplined concentration to the *rules* of the Law. They looked at the common sinners as undisciplined and unwilling to be as righteous, holy and upright as they were. Their lives were all about keeping the regulations of the Law. It was in those regulations, the Pharisees thought, that they would find their acceptance by God as holy men.

But Jesus repeatedly took the legalists (Pharisee and Scribes) to task because of their snotty, arrogant, self-righteous attitudes. Jesus would constantly come to the sinner's defense, so much so that in Luke 11:46, He accused the legalists by saying, *"[W]hat sorrow also awaits you experts in religious law! For you crush people with unbearable religious demands, and you never lift a finger to ease the burden."* More than anything else, it was their double standard, their attitude of superiority that angered Him. Jesus became so angry by their hypocrisy that in Matthew 23, He hit them with a volley of "woes" (sorrows awaiting you ... seven to be exact). There's no question that Jesus was upset at these religious leaders because of their lack of humility and compassion toward God's greatly beloved people. Yes, a number of those people were reprobate and not serving God, but that didn't mean that God loved them less. Jesus was here now to help turn them to God in a new way, a way much different than they had been taught, a way of agape (unconditional) love. So Jesus spit some fire and brimstone on these hypocrites for misrepresenting who God really is and what He had come to accomplish (for all sinners) through the soon-to-be sacrifice that He would pay for all mankind.

(Matt 23:31–33) *"Therefore you are witnesses against yourselves that you are sons of those who murdered the prophets. Fill up, then, the measure of your fathers' guilt. Serpents, brood of vipers! How can you escape the condemnation of hell?"*

Just because Jesus spoke to the legalists this way didn't at all mean that he was trying to diminish the Law. It wasn't that Jesus was condoning living without restraint when it came to behavior, because He wasn't. He's pretty clear on His views of the Law in Matthew 5:17–18.

"Don't misunderstand why I have come. I did not come to abolish the law of Moses or the writings of the prophets. No, I came to accomplish their purpose. I tell you the truth, until heaven and earth disappear, not even the smallest detail of God's law will disappear until its purpose is achieved."

This is a really strong statement by Jesus for the validity of the Law, but we would be wrong to come to the conclusion that Jesus promoted legalism. What He was saying here was that He supported the purpose of the Law so that it would guide and correct behavior. However, He is not saying that the Law is a checklist of rules and regulations by which if we do them, it shows our righteousness before God. Jesus' key statement here is; *"I did not come to abolish the law of Moses or the writings of the prophets. No, I came to accomplish their purpose."* Frankly, He *was* the better way. The Law was only a shadow in comparison to what Jesus had come to give humanity. Jesus came

Calvary Baptist
noappetite pouring

to institute *grace.* The Law was a whip keeping you in line. This is where the legalists find themselves in the church today, even though they may bristle at the mention of them being called the "whip."

Being a judgmental, hypocritical "law is all" person was not popular with Jesus. He couldn't stand this kind of attitude and was explicitly clear about it in Matthew 23. Jesus pours it on the Law guys, particularly in verses 33–34. I like the Message version when reading this. It's in "living, Jesus color!"

33–34 *"Snakes! Reptilian sneaks! Do you think you can worm your way out of this? Never have to pay the piper? It's on account of people like you that I send prophets and wise guides and scholars generation after generation—and generation after generation you treat them like dirt, greeting them with lynch mobs, hounding them with abuse.*

Clearly Jesus isn't pulling any punches about how he feels regarding pious, sanctimonious, religious people. It's because of the legalists trying to get people to "work" at God accepting them that dug at Jesus' crawl. Grace is not *working* or *doing* penance so that God will then approve and accept us. Grace is *knowing* you are loved by God to the extent that when you sin (and you do), God is there holding you securely from the clutches of hell because of the finished work of Jesus on the cross. Damn the theological mentality that says that you have to *work* for God's acceptance in order to fully receive His approval and love. That's the biggest lie from the pit of hell that ever was!

Equally it's important that we should also look at ourselves. Who are we to think that because legalists are so pious and hypocritical that we somehow can't be the same way toward them? That's something that nonlegalists tend to struggle with as well ... the "I'm a step up from you" mentality. If we succumb to that, then really we're no different from the legalist. The feeling of superiority is both seductive and deceptive. John Maxwell said, *"There are two kinds of pride, both good and bad. 'Good pride' represents our dignity and self-respect. 'Bad pride' is the deadly sin of superiority that reeks of conceit and arrogance."* A sense of superiority, conceit, and arrogance stinks in the nostrils of God no matter who the person is. It would do those of us well who take Biblical issue with religious legalists to always be on guard so as to not fall into the same arena of judgment as they do … resulting in becoming one of them.

Pharisaical Attitudes and Actions

Dr. Gary Tyra writes in his book, *Defeating Pharisaism*, about the manner in which the Gospels portray Jesus confronting the Pharisees. He suggests Jesus had a tremendous problem with the Pharisees' tendency toward:

Egoism (self-righteousness and spiritual arrogance) — Some Pharisees tended to be so "confident of their own righteousness" that they looked down on everybody else (Luke 18:9–14).

Dogmatism / Sectarianism — Some Pharisees tended to assume without question that their doctrinal positions were the epitome of absolute truth and that their party alone enjoyed God's approval (Luke 7:29–35; John 9:24–34).

Super-Spirituality / Hyper-Piety — Some Pharisees tended to parade their piety about publicly, drawing attention to their super-scrupulous observance of religious rituals and spiritual disciplines to gain the attention and admiration of their peers (Matthew 6:1, 2, 5, 16; 23:5–7).

Mockery of Christ's wisdom

Traditionalism / Ritualism — Some Pharisees tended to deify human traditions, with the result that they became so overly concerned with a proper engagement in religious customs that they ended up substituting a real relationship with God with a feverous devotion to various religious rituals (Mark 7:1–13).

Legalism / Separatism — Some Pharisees tended to believe that a right relationship with God could be achieved and maintained by mere human effort and by isolating themselves from everyone who did not share their commitment to ritual purity (Matthew 9:10–13; Luke 15:1–32; John 5:39, 40).

Judgmentalism — Some Pharisees tended to behave in harsh, unloving, ungracious, judgmental ways toward anyone who did not belong to their group or whose piety did not match their own (John 8:3–11; 9:13–34).

Pugilism — Some Pharisees tended to believe they were doing God a service by actually persecuting those who might succeed at promoting a religious perspective that differed from their own (Matthew 23:29–34).

Trivialism — Some Pharisees tended to "strain out gnats" while "swallowing camels." They tended to focus all of their attention and emotional energy on trivial issues that lacked scriptural support while ignoring those matters that, according to the Bible, mean a great deal to God (Matthew 23:23, 24).

Formalism / Hypocrisy — Some Pharisees tended to pose and posture — to pretend to be more spiritually mature than they really were (Matthew 23:25–28).

As you can see in Dr. Tyra's above explanation, the behavioral traits of Pharisees in Jesus' day isn't necessarily all that different from the holiness, legalistic Pharisees of today.

Free at Last

Legalism is a favorite weapon of the enemy. If he can arrange for us to be trained under a legalistic teaching and then have us act out in a legalistic manner as well as size people up with a legalistic eye, then we've hit the trifecta of a legalistic life. The enemy couldn't be more pleased. This kind of religious heaviness can actually snuff the flame of Christ's message of grace out of a believer. This is what happened in Galatia and was a major reason for the apostle Paul to write a letter to them (Galatians 5:13–26).

These were a bunch of young, fired up Christians in love with Jesus who started out great in terms of the original teaching that Paul had given them. But as time went on, word got back to Paul that these believers were beginning to become quite legalistic and it was now affecting their group. What started out as a lovefest of agape, grace, and mercy on their road to living a righteous life was now becoming a sect of apathetic religious legalists. Now their hard and legalistic manner was causing them a diminishing of God's Spirit in their lives.

There it is. That's exactly what the influence of legalism does to a person. It minimizes the power of the cross and the redemptive grace that it brings to a person on their life journey. This prevailing spirit of religious legalism sucks the very life out of a believer, or potential believer, because of its grim reaper mentality. Consequently, the free gift of grace provided for us on the cross turns into a hard working job that we have to perform *meticulously* every day of our lives just to barely pay the interest on our salvation. Now that's just a pile of you know what!

Actually, it's really not so much an issue of "Law vs Grace," but rather it's about the *truth* of what Paul tells us in Romans 8:2: "*And*

163

because you belong to him, the power of the <u>life-giving Spirit</u> has freed you from the <u>power of sin</u> that leads to death."

It's because of the torturous sacrifice that Jesus paid on the cross that has provided the "life-giving Spirit" (His Spirit…God's Spirit) that has FREED us from the power of SIN…that death monster that caused Adam to fall and, consequently, all of us as well. Because of Jesus, it's no longer about "working" to be righteous, it's about receiving, accepting, and living in His "life-giving Spirit"—the great antidote for *"the law of sin and death."*

Our faith walk with the Messiah isn't based on the amount of grueling work that a person has to put into it in order to be "righteous." Rather, it's an intimate relationship of agape (love) based on His absolute, unconditional forgiveness of our human flaws (sins) that He paid for on the cross. And, in return, our desire is to lessen those flaws as we daily grow in His glorious image by the power of His Holy Spirit. The Psalmist David described this kind of relationship as "Deep calls to deep" (Psalms 42:7). The deep intimate longing of the *creation* for the *Creator.*

In describing the fraud of legalism, Tim Keller, pastor of Redeemer Presbyterian Church in New York City, said, *"Legalism is looking to something besides Jesus Christ in order to be acceptable and clean before God."*

There is no price that humanity can pay, no act of righteousness that we can perform that would provide for us acceptability before God other than the shed blood of Jesus Christ our Savior. This is the reason legalism doesn't work. There it is, packaged, wrapped, and ready to be sent to the front door of your heart.

10

THE REVELATION OF ME

"The first step toward change is awareness. The second step is acceptance."

Thirdstep is — **Nathaniel Branden, PhD**

want it + fourth step is fight for it,

As a crisis marriage therapist, I often have couples coming into my office with the intent of wanting me to fix the "other" person in order for the relationship to work. Though there are some cases where it's more one person with the issues than the other, still both people usually carry enough baggage into the relationship to make it equitable and interesting. It's often concerning when one or the other, or even just an individual unmarried person refuses to see *his or her* issues. This is when it mostly contributes to the breakdown in relationship[s]. Let me be blunt here. When this occurs in a person, they often are not assuming personal responsibility, but rather they are being selfish and self-centered in their dealings with other strugglers. All of us cracked, clay pots are on a level playing field with God when it comes to our fallen, messed-up state. There are a number of reasons why we fall short in being more successful in maintaining relationships. The old Hymn, *"Ain't my mother, ain't* *my sister, but it's <u>me</u>, O Lord, standin' in the need of prayer"* will go a long way here in looking at the next five points.

The Great Me Revelation #1

The first me revelation is: *in the end, life really isn't just about me and the way that I have assessed and concluded things.* You may see things one way and someone else, especially if it's your partner, may see it another way. If I'm not open to take a look at me *first* before coming to a conclusion in a relational difference, then really what I'm demanding is for the other person to just have enough sense to capitulate and realize that I'm right...ALWAYS...or at least mostly. If this is usually the case, then can you say *narcissist?*

What do you see? Do you see an old woman with a feather in her hair, or a young woman wearing a feather in her hat? One truth but there are two ways to view it.

If you insist on only one way of looking at an issue relationally, then you're missing the full truth, as well as minimizing the other person's insight.

The following is a common example of a number of acute marital cases I've had throughout the years.

Joe and Loretta came to me for some marital counseling claiming that their marriage was in terrible trouble and needed help. They were right. Both Joe and Loretta tended to lean on the "strong-willed" side, so being preferential to each other wasn't necessarily a stellar quality in either of them. Joe could be a compulsive person who dealt with numbers all day for a living. Consequently, things had to be pretty much perfect in order for him to have a good feel in life. Joe was also opinionated as well as preferred structure over chaos when it came to his office at work and at home. Joe's obsession for structure provided for him calm, but for Loretta, their two twin sons and for Joe's coworkers, it could be a challenge when around him. Joe came from a family system that showed a great deal of affection and affirmation. As a result, Joe required as much from Loretta, but when she didn't show it, which was often, Joe became upset and distant. Joe's deep need for affection and affirmation often dominated his world, and because he didn't receive much of that at home, he would tend to compensate for it at work. Whenever others would give him an "attaboy" for his job performance, he would feast on it and even feel a little drawn to them because of their acknowledging his talents and qualities…something he felt Loretta didn't give him. Joe was sensitive, caring, and talented but very insecure.

On the other hand, Loretta was a compulsive person as well, but her compulsions were aimed in other directions like obsessively washing clothes when they had hardly been worn, or possibly, had not been worn at all. However, when approached by Joe or others about her "issue," Loretta was in denial about it and insisted that the need to wash was just that, "a need" and not an obsession. But as far as everyday *structure* (tardiness, neatness, meals being on time, etc.) is concerned, this was not something that bothered her. Loretta's family system was different from Joe's. Though she clearly knew that both her mom and dad loved her very much, still, as far as *overt* expressions of affection and affirmation went, these were things that were few and far between for her growing up. Also, Loretta was employed in law enforcement, and the very nature of her job tended to make her lean on the nonsympathetic, nonaffectionate side. This only compounded the issue because of Joe's needs. Joe couldn't understand why Loretta just wouldn't give him more of these two much needed qualities in their relationship, and Loretta just couldn't understand why Joe required so much of them in order to be satisfied in their relationship. So a battle of the wills ensued… the irreversible force against the immovable object. The eighteen-year hardheaded battle had taken its toll on their relationship. Now it was either do or die… so in came Joe and Loretta for counseling.

As we began working together, I asked Joe and Loretta to please remember one word throughout our sessions, *ownership*. I shared with them that even though they clearly heard the word, it would be the number one word that they would constantly forget as we proceed in therapy. You see, assuming personal ownership (first) rather than immediately projecting the assumed fault on the other person first is both an act of selflessness as well as humility. Unless I take a hard look at *me* and the issues that I carry first, then you're going to have to assume ownership not only first, but always. That means I'm right and you're wrong, not exactly an ingredient for a meaningful, significant, and passionate relationship.

Joe and Loretta continued in therapy for several months. And yes, because of their stubborn natures they forgot the word *ownership* a number of times, and yes, I reminded them of it more times than they forgot. But they were open and brave enough to assume ownership first *before* projecting the fault onto the other.

To avoid personal ownership or responsibility has a certain seductive appeal to it. If, more than not, it's the other person's inability to be able to see it your way, the right way, then that's their problem not yours... right? If you pretend to not be in control while at the same time minimizing the other person's opinion or position on a subject, then that's their problem for having a weak defense... right? If you've convinced yourself that your flaws and relational inadequacies somehow lie outside of the person that you really are, then your ego can remain safe. This then creates a life template for you to run from anything other than what *you* feel is right, therefore building an "It's all about me shield" while falsely defending the opposite.

This isn't at all the approach that any of us should take when interacting with others in life. Acting out in this way actually only shows the longing for control and the total disregard for true personal responsibility. It also shows you just how incredibly insecure you really are by having to blame and guilt others into agreeing with you so as to stroke your overinflated self-opinion.

Let's be honest: even if we set out trying to look at ourselves objectively, the best of our natural self-centered instincts all point us to deflecting to the other person. And not only do we try feverishly to avoid any bad news about ourselves, we also tend to exaggerate the good news.

We self-deceptively think, *When I mess up, it's normally for a good reason. But when other people mess up, it's because, well, they're mess-ups.*

Taking a hard objective look at yourself isn't the easiest thing....
Trust me, I know. We assess, conclude, and then dig in our heels. It
seems and feels right at the time but in reality, it's just a smoke screen
to hide our own insecurity of not wanting to be wrong.

Author and psychologist Dr. Lynne Namka said, *"Wanting and
insisting on getting your own way is a setup for unhappiness. Rigidity in
thinking leads to power struggles...."*

Well, ain't that the truth! To give up our predetermined
conclusions about our inflated self-perception can not only provide
endless opportunities relationally speaking but also can provide the
ingredient for a more balanced view of us.

The Psalmist David said it best in Psalms 139:23–24:

"Search me, O God, and know my heart; (not disciplined)
test me and know my anxious thoughts. (can't trust)

*Point out anything in me that offends you,
and lead me along the path of everlasting life."*

The Great Me Revelation #2

church! church! church

The second me revelation is: *I'm a living product of two very significant
players in my life—temperament and family systems/learned behavior.*
One element is *genetic;* the other is *environmental.* Between the two,
they define the sum of how I act and how I'm seen. These two
components, I believe, are the best indicators of human behavior
that we will ever experience in life.

at salvation @ 16

Ruth Williams- nice but fearful

The (Five) Temperament Types

The Greek physician Hippocrates (c. 460—c. 370 BC) known as the
father of medicine as well as psychology, founded and incorporated

no need for prayer to be born again already are

the four temperaments into his medical theories as part of the ancient medical concept. Today, the four original temperament types are used in (genetic) personality testing by psychologists and mental health professionals around the world.

In 1984, a fifth temperament type was discovered by Drs. Richard and Phyllis Arno, called "supine." The Supine temperament type is characterized by a tendency toward indirect behaviors and an inability to initiate. The Supine is of a gentle nature and often find it difficult to say *no* to people. This fifth temperament type is beginning to be used more and more today in the professional counseling and mental health profession.

> *It should be noted here that if there were <u>not</u> a fifth temperament type (Supine), then this person would tend to fall into the *Melancholy* group.

Temperament is broken up into three categories:

Inclusion: communication, expression, and socialization
Control: decision making, taking on responsibilities
Affection: showing love and affection (emotional connection)

Below are the basic characteristics of the *five* temperament types.

Sanguine

Strengths:

- Optimistic / Lively
- Friendly / Compassionate
- Social / Talkative
- Fun-Filled / Carefree
- People person / Warm

childhood

Weaknesses:
- Tends to interrupt (not the best listeners)
- Temper tantrums (emotional, crying… yell)
- Great starters / Slow finishers / Forgetful
- Unaware of time
- Lustful (pleasure-seeking)

Melancholy

Strengths:
- Task oriented
- Set high standards
- Gifted (arts… design… mechanics, etc.)
- Financially responsible (Frugal)
- Deep thinkers (Analytical)
- Practical (not extravagant)

Adult

Weaknesses:
- Critical/Moody / Not very sociable
- Negative/Shows little affection
- Introverted/Perfectionist
- Is not very talkative
- Fear of Economic Failure

Choleric

Strengths:
- Personable / Active / Passionate
- Charming / High energy / Aggressive
- Inspiring / Crusaders against injustices
- Born Leaders / Dogged determination

Weaknesses:

- Strong-willed / Opinionated
- Self-sufficient / Could lack compassion
- Hot tempered / Impatient
- Domineering
- Impetuous / Headstrong
- Controlling / Bossy

Phlegmatic

Strengths:

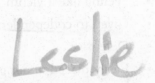

- Sensitive / Calm
- Imaginative / Witty
- Sympathetic / Thoughtful
- Gentle / Kindhearted / Caring
- Intuitive / Feeling-based
- Peacemakers / Easygoing
- Considerate / Patient

Weaknesses:

- Vulnerable / Emotional
- Stubborn
- Fearful / Sad
- Grudge holders (unforgiving)
- Sharp with words

Supine

Strengths:

- Optimistic / Caring
- Gentle spirit

- Upbeat / Servant's heart
- Sensitive / Accommodating
- Supportive / Faithful friend
- Compassionate / Team player

Weaknesses:

- Nonassertive / Withdrawn (wants to express but doesn't)
- Difficulty saying NO
- Feeling like a victim
- Given to codependency / A pleaser (to a fault)
- Defensive
- Easily placed under guilt / easily offended

Temperament is very significant when looking at the *revelation of me*. Why? If I don't factor in my inborn genetic tendencies, both my strengths and weaknesses, then everyone with whom I interact will just have to adapt to me rather than me owning my *stuff*.

It's our temperament that makes some of us art and music lovers while others are sports or industry-minded. Inborn genetic temperament sets broad and defining guidelines on everyone's behavioral patterns. These behaviors will influence a person as long as he or she lives. Each temperament has its own unique qualities, shortcomings, strengths, and challenges. These human behaviors are the way we communicate, interact socially with others, show our responsibility levels, how we take on and make decisions, and how we operate with emotions and affection.

To comprehend temperament more effectively, it's important to understand that the five temperament types are not just an arbitrary collections of different characteristics. They come from a springboard of various interactive dimensions of our human behavior.

fall of humanity everyone is on the same playing field... don't single yourself out or

Isn't it interesting that some people talk about reality while others talk about ideas? Some people do what works, while others do what's right. Then there are those who look at things practically while others dream. Really, the bottom line is each person has the choice, through the power of the Holy Spirit, to develop his or her natural temperament strengths as well as overcome their natural temperament weaknesses. To whatever degree this is accomplished depends on the individual's motivation, their willingness to look at themselves, and the dimension of their faith.

Temperament is *inborn*. It comes from our genetic linage. Therefore it cannot be exchanged for another temperament. You just can't say, "Well, I don't want to be Melancholy any more so I think I'll just start acting like a Sanguine." It just doesn't work that way because temperament is *genetic*. Therefore it's impossible to be something other than what you were born to be. Again, that doesn't mean that with the help of the Holy Spirit you can't learn to get better regarding the negative parts of your temperament. Without question you can. Through Christ each of us can always become stronger so as to sizably overcome the "Adam" part of our temperament. If that wasn't true, then the work of Christ was in vain and ineffective. Know this if nothing else. When it comes to your temperament, because of what the power of the cross has provided for us, all things, in terms of disciplining this body and soul is possible. "*I can do everything through Christ who gives me strength.*" (Phil. 4:13)

Family Systems /Learned Behavior

Another factor of both how I act and how I'm perceived by others is directly linked to what is known as our *family of origin*. This looks *emotionally alone + private* *Dad - Wasn't emotionally available conflicted internally*

at how we can act out, respond or react in social/family settings, and how we emotionally deal with external/internal conflict. Our Family of Origin dates back to Adam and Eve and the conflict that has ensued in families from that time to this. This concept of family of origin was expanded on by Dr. Murray Bowen (1913–1990), and he called his theory, *family systems*. Dr. Bowen was a cutting-edge psychiatric family therapist, scholar, researcher, clinician, teacher, and writer. He was also founder/director of *The Bowen Center for the Study of the Family* in Washington, DC.

Bowen family systems theory is a theory of human behavior that views the family as an emotional unit and uses systems thinking to describe the complex interactions in the unit (family). *Systems thinking* is a way of thinking about, and also a language for describing and understanding, the forces and interrelationships that shape the behavior of systems, in this case the nuclear family (Mom, Dad, and siblings). This discipline helps us to see how to change systems more effectively so as to become stronger and more interactively healthy as a family unit, at least where it's possible.

The reason this model is so important with each of us is because we tend to "act out" toward others in a way we have seen and witnessed others act out in our lives, in particular within our *nuclear family* (Mom, Dad, siblings). So if you witnessed Mom and Dad fighting a lot using harsh words, yelling, being critical, cynical, angry, and all around rude toward each other, there is a good likelihood that you may exhibit some of the same behavior toward your spouse. This of course doesn't mean that you will necessarily act out in this way, but there is a good probability that it could happen. Why? It's learned. *from the nuclear family*

The same can be said if you were taught growing up, by way of observation, to not respect women or men by virtue of how you saw Mom and Dad treating each other. You may find yourself feeling that same way toward the opposite sex. Or, if you, while growing up, were hurt physically, emotionally, or psychologically by one of your parents, then there may be the tendency, because of penned up anger, to act out in the same way toward your children. This can even crossover into sexual abuse. If a child, in particular a male, was sexually abused, there is the possibility that the child when he grows up could end up sexually abusing another child or children. Surely not all children who have been sexually abused necessarily become abusers themselves. However, where there is sexual abuse, it's not uncommon for it to be tracked back to the person himself being sexually abused as a child. Whether it's yelling, demeaning language, tone, no regard for patience or listening to the other person, a lack of empathy or sympathy, emotional, physical or sexual abuse, it often comes from learned behavior, something you witnessed, something you experienced. conflict not addressed

Learned behavior is also manifested in other less destructive ways. Example: Sarah is a neat freak who likes everything put in its place as well as a relatively clean and well-groomed house. This is the way she was raised. This is what she witnessed her Mom do, and this is how she and her siblings lived. John, on the other hand doesn't mind a messy house. It isn't really important to him that things are put up and that the house is neat. This is the way he was raised, this is what he witnessed his mom and dad do, and this is how he and his siblings lived. The two stories aren't that much of a big deal until you realize that Sarah and John are married. Because of the huge differences in the way they were brought up, when it comes to domestic structure, it tends to cause friction between them, which in turn creates pressure in their marriage.

abuse led to avoidance

Mom- shutdown (protection)
Alison + Carolyn
skating rink

Learned traits or behavior encompass most of what makes up your personality. When you open the door for someone and you say "please" and "thank you," those are learned behaviors that help you to get along with others, to make friends, or to be caring. When you eat a healthy diet opposed to taking in junk food all the time, that's a learned behavior. If you are more considerate to people than selfish, that can be a learned behavior. Your mannerisms, the way you interact with others, your preference in listening to people more than dominating the conversation, that can be a learned behavior. Your tone, your religious beliefs, your food preferences, and the kind of activities you enjoy are all learned behaviors or traits.

When seeing the need to look at this particular revelation of me—and we should—that would mean taking responsibility for my actions if any of the above issues apply to me ... and you know some of them do.

Family systems and learned behavior issues are real and exist within every person and in every family and have been since the beginning of the human existence. No one is exempt from the emotional pressures and dysfunctional family dynamics that go on in all of us.

handwritten margin notes: diet + exercise; taking responsibility + acting; we all have issues; X

handwritten note: Since dysfunction of Adam + Eve

The Great Me Revelation #3

The third me revelation is: *"I don't mind calling you out on your stuff, but I hate being called out on mine."* Taking responsibility for our "stuff" in life is one of the hardest things for a person to do. It's not natural.

This me revelation is a huge challenge with most if not all of us. Why? We're inherently selfish and not prone to looking at our own stuff (first) before pointing the finger at the other person. This is compounded when you're in a marital relationship. Self-evaluation is

handwritten note at bottom: dysfunctional behavior. It's not just a narrow perspective of yourself. You are not the only sinner!

[handwritten note at top: must face + confront]

a bitter pill to swallow. We'd rather the other person swallow it. That way we can have our cake and eat it too ... without a bitter taste in our mouth.

In Isaiah 6, we see the prophet having this self-discovery of his own human corruption.

"Woe to me!" I cried. "I am ruined! For I am a man of unclean lips, and I live among a people of unclean lips, and my eyes have seen the King, the Lord Almighty."

[handwritten note: I wish Satan was never in the Garden of Eden]

Here's the thing though: he only notices his "ruined" condition because of what proceeded in verses 1–4. Isaiah saw a holy God exalted on a throne with angels around Him, two flying, calling to each other, *"Holy, holy, holy is the Lord Almighty; the whole earth is full of his glory."* Then the doorpost and threshold shook the entire temple and after that, the temple became filled with smoke. Now, tell me, who wouldn't be flipped out to the point of self-evaluation when witnessing this kind of drama?

[handwritten note in right margin: Not what I + choose not my way]

[handwritten note: This is not my choice]

God was calling Isaiah, and apparently everyone else, to look at their own "stuff" without first pointing their finger at someone else. *[handwritten note: God!]* I can't clearly see what God wants to do *for me* until I first allow Him access *in me*. Unless I'm open and willing to give God the keys to my front door, He'll just wait outside until I'm ready to let Him in. That does speak to His endless patience and the great love He has for me, but it also speaks to my selfish attachment to me and the way I want things done.

[handwritten note: The pain and struggle]

Roger and Clair came to me wanting to work on better ways to communicate with each other. She said that Roger always "turns things around" when she comes at him with an issue. He makes it seem that the problem is really *her* and not him. Roger's position was

[handwritten note at bottom: I wish Satan was never created to create all this chaos of sin is too unbearable + ignorance is bliss]

that Clair's issues were not real issues of substance, but rather just nitpicking, mundane things. What she really needs to do is look at herself. Now, there's a backstory here. Remember, there is always a *symptom/cause* when it comes to issues that people have with each other, in particular in marriages, and so it was with Roger and Clair.

Roger, in temperament, was a Choleric in his *Inclusion* (the way he expressed and communicated), Choleric/Phlegmatic in *Control* (decision making and taking on responsibilities), and Sanguine in his *Affection* (emotional expression). Basically Roger could be intimidating in the way he expresses himself to Clair. He's not really open to looking at himself first when Clair approaches him with an issue. He has a tendency to deflect back to her, yet he wanted her to be emotionally connected with him because of his high need for affection. Also, Roger's family systems consisted of a father who was domineering, who overextended his punishments, was opinionated, and was always right. His mother was very loving and doted on him and his siblings but walked a fine line when it came to his dad. She was often very submissive to him.

Clair on the other hand was Melancholy in her *Inclusion*, Supine/Phlegmatic in her *Control*, and Supine in her *Affection*. So Clair's temperament was noticeably different from Roger's. Clair is very logical and practical in the way she both expresses and receives communication. She has no desire to make decisions or dominate others. She can show affection but does not have a high need for it like Roger does. Clair's family systems consisted of a father who was a laid back man, not dominating at all, a cerebral thinker and patient. Her mother had a servant's heart and was also laid back. She could express herself and even get emotional at times if provoked. She was also affectionate, but not overly so. She tended to *internalize* her feelings rather than freely share them.

As a marriage therapist, I had to get Roger to see that Clair is probably often right in thinking that he can "turn things around" when confronted with an issue as well as having the tendency to make things seem that Clair really has more problems than he does. Also he needed to allow her to feel *safe* enough to express her point of view without him shutting her down by turning things around on her. As for Clair, I had to get her to see that her ability to often give in to Roger's intimidation wasn't healthy. She had to learn to stay in the conversation and call Roger out when she feels he's being intimidating. Clair needs to try to connect more in being overtly affectionate to Roger. Roger needs to give Clair reason to want to be more affectionate by listening to her more rather than trying to do a "Jedi mind trick" on her.

It wasn't easy for Roger to see his shortcomings in therapy. He didn't like exposing his *stuff*. He wasn't used to it, and it didn't temperamentally come natural for him. It wasn't something he witnessed growing up. Yet, because Roger loved Clair and was a follower of Jesus, he gradually came around and took more ownership of his challenging behavior. Clair, because of Roger's willingness to look at the way he treated her, became more invested in showing him more affection, attention, and respect. If all of us can catch this revelation of ourselves, wow, would things flow better relationally ... not only with others, but with God as well.

J.M. Barrie, author of the popular book, *Peter Pan*, once said, "*Life is a long lesson in humility.*" Humility is the easiest thing to expect from others and the hardest thing to produce ourselves. Taking responsibility for our *stuff* may not be natural, but it's very effective and rewarding when it comes to relational success.

The Great Me Revelation #4

The fourth me revelation is: *any day can be a day that reaches around and bites you, so… don't think you're all of that!* Being conscious of our weaknesses is a good thing. It keeps us aware of our own fallibility and constant dependence on His grace.

The apostle Paul, someone who knew a thing or two about weaknesses, wisely said to each and every one of us in 1 Corinthians 10:12:

"Don't be so naive and self-confident. You're not exempt. You could fall flat on your face as easily as anyone else. Forget about self-confidence; it's useless. Cultivate God-confidence." (The Message)

Just when you think that you're really doing good in your faith walk, maybe even better than that other Christian who seems to mess up more than not, then take note. You're just a half a breath away from screwing up yourself, according to brother Paul.

If we're not wise enough to take personal inventory of our *overconfidence* in facing life's challenges, then, as Paul was telling the church at Corinth, we could end up falling "flat on [our] faces."

Everyone of us—I don't care how godly you think you are—are open prey for the enemy to try and put us in the wrong place, at the wrong time, under the wrong circumstances, with the wrong people or person. No man or woman is impenetrable. The enemy knows your weakness and your genetic family temperament weaknesses. He even knows the weaknesses that you don't even know you have. He's just waiting for the right opportunity to try to set you up so he can capitalize on the crack in your armor. His complete purpose and reason for existence is to "steal, kill, and destroy" in every created soul of God, to reduce you to fear, guilt, misery, and hopelessness.

Because Jesus Christ had to suffer greatly so if He had to struggle gravely why as His followers shouldn't we?

Believers in Jesus are his prime targets. He'll not only try to make your life personally miserable, but he'll also try to maneuver his way into your marriage, children, extended family, finances, emotional and physical health, faith, relationships, and morals just to mention a few. You might be saying, "Wow, Fred, you make it sound like the grim reaper is living outside my door." No, I'm just trying to get you to smell the coffee when it comes to our absolutely corrupted human condition and how our pathetic *Adam-linked* weakness is open game to the enemy on any given day. When we see that one of our brothers or sisters have fallen into sin in some capacity or that they just aren't walking with God in a way that you think they should, just remember what Paul said, *"You could fall flat on your face as easily as anyone else."* To often take inventory of the chinks in our own armor can be not only wise, but also compassionate toward other fallen mortals.

This is the reason that God not only sacrificed His deeply beloved Son to provide redemption for our sins, but also to give us His beautiful tolerant *grace* to live on until we close our eyes in death. It's this grace and His unfathomable love that is shown to us unlovely ones everyday of our lives on this journey. If these two gifts of God weren't provided for us in the struggle, then we'd be up the (proverbial) "creek without a paddle!" It's that peace of God given to the restless and weary, that undeserved favor from our loving Heavenly Father that stoops down and rescues the broken and the ill-deserving.

Speaker, minister, and author Dr. Justin Holcomb said of grace, *"Grace is most needed and best understood in the midst of sin, suffering, and brokenness. We live in a world of earning, deserving, and merit, and these result in judgment. That is why everyone wants and needs grace. Judgment kills. Only grace makes alive."*

Why did the pain..? Why did Job have to go thru such a painful process??

hanging like Job. He was already faithful to you Why did he need to why prove his faith more OK with you, God wasn't his current state

183

need breakthrough

Yes, the enemy is out to eat our lunch and literally destroy every aspect of us. But God has provided His grace through Christ that shows us His never-ending love and His matchless acceptance of all of us who struggle, yet can struggle well as a result of His promises. Why? Things really do reach around and bite all of us in life, and His grace and unconditional agape provides the healing ointment to keep going, even when going seems rough.

remember His grace and love

The Great Me Revelation #5

The fifth me revelation is: *Even though it's hard to admit, I struggle with forgiving others as well as myself.* It's not an easy thing to honestly acknowledge, but most of us struggle with the whole concept of forgiveness.

The *forgiveness* word has been bothering me since the very beginning of my conversion to Jesus. It's the most emotionally appealing and liberating thing to read about, yet it's the most elusive thing to hold on to when you need to give it out.

Forgiveness is kind of like cleaning out the shed. You know you have to eventually do it, but you just don't want to. I've already highlighted this topic in Chapter 6, so I don't want to belabor this too much. But if I'm not willing to allow the Holy Spirit to help me, probably daily, with my struggle to forgive others, then I'm completely missing out on the very epicenter of God's heart, not to mention the whole theme of the New Testament.

Miroslav Volf said, "*If I say I forgive you, I have implicitly said you have done something wrong to me. But what forgiveness is at its heart is both saying that justice has been violated and not letting that violation count against the offender.*" That's really the struggle now, isn't it? How can

prodigal daughter

you need to receive and so do others forgiveness

especially from judgmental church

I both acknowledge the injustice I suffered from you while letting go of that injustice at the same time? Now that's a tall glass of water!

I think it's because forgiveness isn't just about "I've got to do this because Jesus says I must," as much as it's about character, discipline, understanding, benevolence, humility, empathy, and love. As I'm willing to step out on the great forgiveness diving board, what I'm really doing is checking *me* as much as I'm letting go. Matter of fact, you can really only effectively forgive (let go) if you're open and willing to allow the above attributes to be formed in you. We're not inherently born with these qualities. They are built within us over time through adversity, self-examination, and testing.

All of us struggle with unforgiveness because it's the most powerful weapon in the enemy's arsenal for separation. Its goal is to "divide and conquer." God's goal, however, is to unite and release with obedience through grace. As we do this, we release our pain and anger that only cripples and paralyzes us from being better than what we can be.

Forgiving Ourselves

Forgiving yourself is absolutely essential if you are to be free from the emotions attached to the offence. There's a tendency in many of us to hold ourselves more accountable than we do with others. Perhaps it's easier for you to justify forgiving others, yet you find no justification for forgiving yourself for an equal or lesser offense. Maybe you believe that forgiving yourself is not even a consideration because you think you have to hold yourself in a state of constant remembrance, lest you forget. Or perhaps you even believe there's a price, some form of lifelong penance that you must pay for your offence. It's a belief system about personal forgiveness that we have to break in order to reap the many benefits that forgiveness has to offer us.

The apostle Peter said in Acts 10:34, *"I now realize how true it is that God does not show favoritism."* When it comes to knowing God or Him forgiving us, we have to understand that God does not choose to forgive one person and not another. He forgives everyone who believes in Jesus, His Son. If we're applying His "no partiality" standards to others, then it has to be equally as important to forgive ourselves.

Forgiving others and even yourself is not about forgetting, nor is it about excusing the offence, but rather, it's about dealing with the anger and resentment you have toward the person[s] who have offended you as well as crawling out from under the condemnation and guilt that you've placed on yourself. Forgiving yourself is *letting go* of what you are holding on to against yourself. It's accepting and living in His beautiful and undeserved grace so as to experience the wonder and lavishness of His endless and passionate love for us. They both go hand in hand. If God has forgiven our sin[s] and moved on, shouldn't we do the same and move on with Him?

When we reject the forgiveness extended to us by God through Christ, when we refuse to forgive ourselves, what we're really doing is setting ourselves above others, and that's simply pride. Now, in saying that, if a person has an ongoing problem of forgiving themselves, then there may be some specific reasons just why this is happening. In such cases, counseling with a professional licensed Christian counselor could prove very helpful.

Encompassing a larger revelation and understanding of myself, not only my assets but my deficits as well, can be the difference between soaring with the birds or being under them after they've eaten a meal. Catch the picture?

11

EMBRACING THE GRAY

"Man — a creature made at the end of the week's
work when God was tired."

— Mark Twain

Chris Rohan, *Abilities Expo ambassador and former publisher of*
Disabled Dealer Magazine writes:

When Annie Hopkins and her brother Stevie incorporated 3E
Love in 2007, the wheelchair heart or "International Symbol of
Acceptance" became the company's trademark and the drive behind
much of its goals and products. It is a symbol of society accepting
people with disabilities as equals and a symbol that people with
disabilities accept their challenges and even embrace them. Annie
felt that by replacing the wheel with a heart, the stigma of the
wheelchair is also removed, and it can be a symbol for people with
any disability or impairment. It represents the person, not society's
perception of him or her.

The wheelchair heart is the attitude and a lifestyle that Annie
epitomized. She encouraged others to accept their abilities, rally
around that diversity, and turn it into strength. Her graphic creation

inspired others to love and live life to the fullest no matter who you are and what you look like, no matter what you can or cannot do.

"3E Love is more than living disabled, it is simply about living. Everyone has the freedom to live their life. We challenge you to do what you love, because you'll meet some amazing people along the way, and that, our friends, is how you'll enjoy this ride that 3E Love calls, life," Annie said.

Annie Hopkins was twenty-four years old when she died in 2009, of complications from spinal muscular atrophy. She was a graduate student in the disability studies master program at University of Illinois at Chicago.

Facing What It Is

The cool thing about reading Annie Hopkin's story was how she not only learned to accept her disabilities, but she "embrace[d]" them as well. This brave, gifted, and successful entrepreneur didn't enter into denial and self-pity about her physical limitations. Rather, she embraced them and even used them as a springboard to accomplish her goal of launching 3E Love.

Annie faced *what it is*. As far as she was concerned, her disabilities were real, they were what they were. What was she going to do about it? Can something positive and influential come from something, in this case someone, with limited physical and physiological abilities? Well, with Annie Hopkins, the answer was obviously … yes!

But within our evangelical Christian community, I've found that a number of believers just find it difficult to wrap their minds around an honest look at our human *fallen* limitations. Many feel that to look at their limitations (sin struggles) is then to agree with Satan that we really have them. NEWS FLASH: we do! A lot of people in the church believe that they have to constantly live up to a "yardstick of rules" in order to please God, consequently voiding out the reality of our struggling fallen state. It's this Pharisaic prevailing attitude within the church that says we can't *really* serve Jesus nor can we stack up to a Holy God in these fallen corrupted spacesuits. That somehow we can't *struggle* and be used of God at the same time. That we constantly have to "prove" ourselves to God in order for Him to use us. It's the Matthew 5:48 indictment, *"Be perfect, therefore, as your heavenly father is perfect."* It's not only the misinterpreting and misunderstanding of this scripture, it's also the whole evangelical narrow-minded way of thinking that misrepresents it.

In looking at this in the *Message*, it throws out a clearer idiomatic structure of the language in question.

"In a word, what I'm saying is, Grow up. You're kingdom subjects. Now live like it. Live out your God-created identity. Live generously and graciously toward others, the way God lives toward you."

Not "perfect" in the sense of being free of mistakes or shortcomings but rather "grow up" to a place, a goal of "God-created identity." It's an ongoing life that's not free of human struggles. We are called to Kingdom live in our relationship with God and, frankly, that takes a lifetime of experiencing both spiritual success and embracing the *gray* of human struggle. This is the handicap part of us, the difficult part. Because of the consequences of the Fall, these two go together... good life experiences and bad. We can't escape them. There are times of rejoicing and tears, clarity and obscurity, stability and uncertainty, confidence and doubt. You can't have one life experience without the other. There is no feeling the elation of success unless there was first the experience of failure. We are both blessed as well as cursed. We have a God who *"is able, through his mighty power at work within us, to accomplish infinitely more than we might ask or think"* (Ephesians 3:20). Yet He is doing that very thing in us through our fallen, sinful, corrupted humanity. Will we ever really comprehend His remarkable love and omnipotent power? Let's just be honest and say no.

By us being honest with our struggling through *the gray* doesn't at all mean that we're without help or hope. It's just a visceral and transparent look at the way we all really are...flawed and broken. That's right. We were all born messed up and with issues...ALL of US! But when you factor in the redemption of the cross along with the power of the Holy Spirit mixed with the beauty of the Father's forgiveness, there lies our hope to forge through the gray to a place of peace and rest, yes, even through the struggle.

But who hasn't had their life's colors mixed to gray at times? Who hasn't had their hearts broken or have felt that God must have turned a deaf ear to their prayers? Were you wondering if you had to carry this burden[s] for the rest of your life? Who hasn't felt disappointment and pain at times while walking with God? Listen to King David's desperate cry in Psalms 28:1–2 (*The Message*):

> Don't turn a deaf ear
> when I call you, God.
> If all I get from you is
> deafening silence,
> I'd be better off
> in the Black Hole.
>
> I'm letting you know what I need,
> calling out for help

And lifting my arms
toward your inner sanctum.

David knew both the spiritual delight of worship as well as the sweet intimacy of relationship with God. Yet he was as human as any of us and had his moments of disappointment and sadness in his walk with the Father. In reality, the cute little Christian sound bites that say, "God said it, I believe it, that settles it," or "You may have failed, but God didn't," or "It's all good," just doesn't always cut it when it feels like you're bare naked in the "valley of the shadow of death." It's in these very places that we meet with God and He with us. Experiencing the mountaintop is a great feel, but our lives are more often lived out in the low places. It's the place that God told Adam was a *cursed ground*, a place of *painful toil, thorns, thistles,* and *sweat*, and a place that will eventually open up and take him back from where he was formed (Genesis 3:17–19). That's the gray that finds itself attached to each of us at some point in our life. It may be in the sadness and questioning of a Mom and Dad whose child is dying of cancer, the heartache and codependency fight of parents with a drug addicted son or daughter, the deep grieving over a spouse that has died after forty years of marriage, the battling with God over the confusion of sexual identity, or the constant praying that the mental health issue that you struggle with will go away when it never does. This is the gray filtered through the grace of God that keeps us all moving forward even when moving forward seems too monumental to conceive.

Embracing the gray isn't saying that I agree with it or will even give into it. It is saying, however, that it's there, it exists, and it has somehow found its way to my front door, my life, my world. To deny the gray in our lives is to deny reality, and to ignore reality is to limit our options for success.

Really, It's Unconditional

If you find yourself being unproductive in life, whether that's with work, relationships, family, mood, personal motivation, or faith, then there is a real likelihood that you're depressed. This can be a part of the *gray*. A lot of people will feel guilty about this to the point where they're constantly beating up on themselves, either that or they've just stopped caring. For the believer, the world of "I just don't care" and the voice of the Holy Spirit saying, *"Rejoice in the Lord always"* can be two very contrasting and at times torturing mentalities. It's right here at this time in our lives that we must seek to understand the matchless unconditional, unchanging love that God has for us in Christ. It's only in the welcome acceptance of His *agape* love that we're able to feel lifted out of the guilt and self-deprecation that comes with the experience of depression. It's the ploy of the enemy that makes us feel that our value and worth in the eyes of God only comes out of what we can produce. God doesn't ask us to *produce* anything in order for Him to love and accept us more. God really only requires three things of us according to Micah 6:8: *"To act justly and to love mercy and to walk humbly with your God."* And even with these He doesn't say, *If you don't do them as you should, I won't love you.*

We have to catch the full dynamic of what the apostle Paul is saying when he powerfully said in (1 Corinthians 13:8), *"Love never fails."* Even in the gray this love can and will sustain you. It transcends through all time and space, in every area of our life, the past, the now, and the future. It breaks through and can level out every neuron, serotonin, dopamine, and biochemical imbalance, and it can redirect every neurotransmitter and nerve cell in your body to operate better. The author of love, God Himself, will not fail to help uplift the depressed with the power of His never-failing agape. Love touches every area of our spirit, soul, and body, and acts as a spiritual and emotional advantage over the gray that tries to claim so many of us. Knowing that you ARE loved by God, truly, unconditionally, and passionately, no matter what state of mind you find yourself in, can provide a peaceful solace that helps transcends your current mental atmosphere. We need to consider treating the gray as not an intruder or a stranger but rather as a family member. You know what I mean. It's kind of like having to calm down your sister when she overreacts to a statement that wasn't intended to cause such an uproar or talking your friend off the ledge when his wife announces she's "had enough and [wants] a divorce!" The feelings, the intensity, the gripping anguish is all there. It's real, and you know you have to address it. But it's more like working with a family member or friend through the struggle than with a stranger. If I treat the gray as an intruder, then I'm going to push away and run from it. But if I look at it as a family member, be it a dysfunctional family member, I won't be so standoffish or prone to have nothing to do with it. It's a little more familiar to me. Therefore it's a little easier to address and give hope to. Knowing that I am deeply loved by my Heavenly Father enables me to forge ahead even though it *feels like* I'm believing against belief, hoping against hope, and trusting against trust. The emotional security that is supplied by truly being loved unrestrictedly and unlimitedly provides the needed sense of hope to continue doing life when continuing seems almost impossible. In connecting with His love in this way, even through the gray, there can still be that distant small voice that says… *"Just one more inch and you'll be there.*" It's that voice that gives a ray of color to an otherwise colorless time in your life.

We are valuable. Even through the depression and anxiety, we have enormous value with God. Matter of fact, "enormous" is even a weak word to describe the endlessly immense and dynamically emotional, unconditional, selfless, and powerful love that God has for us. His love is a force more monumental than any other force known to man. It's in the connecting with and realizing the passion of His love for us that we can find ourselves slipping out of the grip of depression and back into the sunlight of life. His limitless and redemptive love never fails us ... never. It's that amazing!

What I'm suggesting is this: the gray that tries to pull and overtake us through life's battles can often act as a medicine that brings us into emotional balance. Let me explain.

The best way to avoid getting bit by a dog is to stay in one place and NOT run from it. A dog's naturel instinct is to chase you, so staying still is the best way to avoid being bitten. The same thing can be said regarding depression, anxiety, or any other mental health disorder. If you accept it for what it is, don't run from it and learn how to circumvent its bite; you can actually then get better at navigating *through* it rather than running and getting bit *by it*. This can be through meditation and prayer, professional counseling, medication, or all three. As we stand in knowing God's love for us, running from the gray becomes something we do less of and the accepting and navigating through it becomes something we do more of. It really does work if you work it.

We all at some point have struggled with the voice of God assuring us that we have value and are loved unconditionally in the face of our sins that try to convince us otherwise. In a world that so often tells us that our value only comes from what we can do and

[Handwritten margin note, left side:] Yes, this may be all good but not if a Christian doesn't believe it due to distorted teaching

[Handwritten note, bottom:] — God may know all this but I don't and it doesn't help me out....

produce demands a rebuttal that says, "I'd rather weigh my value on the arms of the cross than by the deeds of my hands." Anything less is a gross devaluing of our completed worth in the sight of God the Father.

The gray does its best to try and diminish us to a place of emotional and spiritual reduction. It tries to confirm our disqualification from being used by God as a result of the life struggles we experience. After all, God certainly can't use people who are suffering with grief, depression, anxiety, addiction, moral failure, or any other struggle, can He? The fact is the Bible is riddled with people just like this who not only have been used of God through their flaws, but greatly loved in the process. People like *Abraham*, *Sarah*, *Moses*, *David*, *Jacob*, *Samson*, *Noah*, *Jeremiah*, *Paul*, *Peter*, and *Thomas* just to mention a few. Yes, people who have in the past or presently do live in the gray have great worth, purpose, and value with God. It's the honest gray people who tend to empathize more than those who pretend not to be in the gray and really are.

Rev. Paul Johansson, president emeritus of *Elim Bible Institute and College*, made a very spiritually powerful yet humanly profound statement when he said, *"We've lived in your wounds, Lord, now let us be instruments of your healing."* It's the gray in our lives, the disappointments, weaknesses, and struggles as well as the joys, strengths, and victories that mold us into instruments of healing, broken pots that provide comfort and understanding to other broken pots. It's the fully God and fully man who Isaiah said *"was despised and rejected by mankind, a man of suffering, and familiar with pain."* It's this man, this struggling Savior when He walked this earth that we can relate to when it comes to our earthly misery and heavenly hope.

Life is a struggle, my friend, and as believers in Jesus we struggle through the same life experiences that non-believers do. Being a

Christian doesn't exempt us from personal challenges or emotional pain any more than it does from bacterial infections. In addition to all the struggles common to humanity, we also have the additional struggles of trying to overcome the daily onslaught of sin and being faithful to God's Word in what is becoming a rapidly faithless society. Not complaining here, just a fact. Thank God for the power of the Holy Spirit that was sent down when Jesus ascended. If it weren't for Him, we would be a car without an engine attempting to travel through life!

A Shot of Grace Helps the Gray

Grace is salvage, and God has a way of recycling human salvage to a place of esteem. Actually, our healing begins when we see our pain not as separating us from God but rather connecting us to Him [in the journey] through His great grace and compassionate agape. This is what moves us from the gray into a place of *being* with God. That's why the apostle Paul could say with confidence to the saints at Philippi, *"Grace and peace to you from God our Father and the Lord Jesus Christ."* (Philippians 1:2) Grace is the vehicle that transports us to a location of peace (being) with God. If not, then we would never be able to rid ourselves of the guilt of sin. If we could only connect with the fact that it's not so much that we've sinned—we all sin—but it's how we respond to our human condition in light of the cross that really matters. It's how we walk out our grace-filled journey with the Messiah *through faith* that brings praise to God for His finished work through His Son, Jesus.

It's the *jagged edges* of our humanity that we struggle with at the same time as we wrestle with a Holy God that transforms us into His likeness. It's the lifelong dichotomy of good and evil, right and wrong, peace and restlessness that makes that gray perhaps more of a fight than we would like. This is where the power of God's grace comes in to add balance when our fallen, sinful humanity clashes with God's righteous redemptive love. Jaggedness meets generosity; condemnation meets kindness. This is the antidote for the gray, knowing that you're never disqualified from His love while struggling to seemingly find your way back into His arms...when in reality you were there all the time. There are no obstructions to God's grace, and there are no limits to His Love. The hymn writer Frances J. Crosby said it best when he wrote, *"Oh, the unsearchable riches of Christ, Wealth that can never be told. Riches exhaustless of mercy and grace, Precious, more precious than gold."*

The Art of Listening

It's so easy for many of us to be critical of a person's struggling journey with God. How often are we so quick with answers to questions we really haven't taken time to understand ourselves? People do want answers, but more than that, they just want to know that we're *listening* to them...really listening. Why? If we don't lovingly take the time to listen to our friends who struggle, how will they know that we care? When you're actually listening to someone, you're focusing on "the person," not yourself. Sincerely listening to someone requires a concentrated refusal to be distracted by your own ego and personal agenda. It's asking the Holy Spirit to help you reduce yourself to a place of humility in conversation...not an easy task for most of us. To spell it out plainly, it's about THEM, not you.

After you've taken time to listen, *then* you can ask some questions. It's always good to ask a question before providing an answer. Example: *"Your wife shared with you that she feels unimportant when she's around you. Why do you think she feels that way, Larry?"* It gives Larry time to express his reasoning, and it gives you more information to help him with the answer. Then there are times when people really don't want or need your "wise counsel" at all, they just need your *ear*. There are moments when a caring, *listening ear* is more therapeutic than 10,000 words of good intention. The apostle James had some real insight from God when he said in (1:19); *"Everyone should be quick to listen, slow to speak ...."* One of the most caring, spiritual and loving forms of respect that can be offered to someone is simply *listening* to them.

Often, the art of listening is something that is acquired; it's not automatic. To listen is to pay *specific* attention to the person who is talking to you, and that means NOT interrupting. This becomes a real problem for the person who has ADD or ADHD because for them, every waking moment is an opportunity to talk, particularly if they are *Sanguine* in temperament. Truly listening for the ADD/ADHD person is a foreign experience. Talking and interrupting they know; listening for them is boring and uneventful. To allow a person to be able to speak without interruption is as rare as an honest politician. In walking through the gray in life, to just have a few people as a sounding board to bounce feelings off, without the apprehension of being preached to, can be a safe place to receive some comfort. To not interrupt a person as they're sharing some life pain, even when you feel that you have something good to give out, is of itself an act of compassion. As you're listening, it also allows the Holy Spirit to sift through the gray to help offer to the person some perspective that may lead to a little ray of hope. The goal is to shine the flashlight on them, not you, to listen to their story, not for you to tell them yours.

The art of listening is to be able to listen without forming responses in your mind, to listen and not have five things rolling around in your cranium that you just can't wait to get out. Try to listen to everything that they have to say, not anxiously waiting for "the comma" so you can quickly add your two cents, but rather being sensitive to their "period" … when they're finished.

Listening is also about *nonverbal* communication. About 60 to 70 percent of our communication that we give out is nonverbal. That's a huge percentage! In order to know when to speak and when to pause in the listening process, it's very important to understand what the person's body language is saying. Do they seem hesitant, sad, wounded, or untrusting? Do they show positive signs like appearing relaxed, making eye contact, and engaging in conversation? Or are they throwing out negative signs like leaning away from you, crossing their arms, or looking from side to side? These are all signs that can be helpful in discovering the art of listening.

The Greek philosopher, Diogenes Laertius, said: *"We have two ears and only one tongue in order that we may hear more and speak less."* To be part of the graduating class of "The Art of Listening," there has to be a longing in you to be reduced (humbled) to the place of *"them first and me last."* Listening is a rare yet invaluable life skill that when accomplished, can be a real contributing source of healing to the person who just needs an ear. Also, the bonus takeaway here is not only will it help you to be more sensitive to others, it will benefit you as well when interacting with friends and family. It's a success tool that keeps on giving in every area of your life.

Man's a Mess

Mark Twain was humorously right in my beginning quote of this chapter when he said, *"Man—a creature made at the end of the week's work when God was tired."* Twain indicates the brokenness and fallibility of these human vessels. It's kind of like when we joke about never wanting to buy a car that was built on a *Friday*, when people had worked all week and were tired and ready to go home. *The gray* has been genetically slammed into each one of us by virtue of the Fall. Whether not often depressed, sometimes depressed, or clinically depressed, we all have stared into the gray at some point in our lives, and if you haven't, you will. Life just does that to you.

The psalmist David penned it best: *"And me? I'm a mess. I'm nothing and have nothing...."* Psalms 40:17 (*The Message*)

In the end, we're all "a mess." We came into this world with nothing, and that's exactly how we're going to leave it. The gray was the direct result of narcissistic disobedience on the part of God's first human creation. What followed after that was a catastrophic failure that completely decimated man's ability to think, act, and feel anything other than what is first good for him. That thought pattern has taken its devastating toll on everything from defining morality to the destruction of human life in countless ways. The human failure effect has even influenced political thought patterns throughout the world, in a more personal way, right here in our country of the United States. That kind of influence can play a heavy part in the gray seeping into an otherwise already emotionally taxed state of mind. As Dr. Allan Bloom wrote in his book, *The Closing of the American Mind:* "Enlightenment killed God; but like Macbeth, the men of the Enlightenment did not know that the cosmos would rebel at the deed, and the world became 'a tale told by an idiot full of sound and fury,* *signifying nothing.'"* That statement sounds very much like the empty teachings of our secular universities and colleges today. This is the reason we so need to connect with the authority of God, redemption through His Son, Jesus, and the leading, sensitivity, and power of the Holy Spirit. Why? The *reason* is that man cannot find God; only the Holy Spirit can find God for man. But because man is inherently selfish and self-centered, he has reasoned away God, thus the idiot[s] "full of sound and fury, signifying nothing."

Everyone affects someone and everything affects something. The gray is like throwing a stone into a pond. It's rippling effect starts small but eventually ends up reaching all the way to the shoreline. Whether those affects reach you personally through marital pressures, the loss of a loved one, financial issues, life's sneak-ups, spiritual questioning, or political discouragement, the gray is only sized for one containment box, God.

Martin Luther said, *"I have held many things in my hands, and I have lost them all; but whatever I have placed in God's hands, that I still possess."* The only lasting thing that we have access to in this struggling life is our faith. Faith crashes through all senselessness, pain, and question and lands in a place that constantly sends out a homing signal that eventually returns us back to our permanent address with God.

The prophet Isaiah called his "gray" out in the open when he said, *"Woe to me!" I cried. "I am ruined! For I am a man of unclean lips, and I live among a people of unclean lips, and my eyes have seen the King, the Lord Almighty."* (Isaiah 6:5) God became more life-giving and transforming to him in light of his acknowledgement of being "ruined" and a "man of unclean lips." He embraced the gray in his life *first* then looked to God to meet him through the struggle.

Embracing the gray in your struggling areas of life doesn't mean that you're a failure. It means that you are honest enough and determined enough to eventually believe for God's favor on the other side of the smoke of battle. It's acknowledging the propensity of your fallen human nature to break down while at the same time somehow holding on to Him who will not fail you.

At the end of the day, it's God or bust! Life's difficulties visit all of us in one form or another. Clouds come in and out of a person's life like the tide, but one thing is for sure: without something to hold steady to during the storm, we're swept away. Whether it's a disorder or a family tragedy, the gray tries to put its claws in us like a tiger on its prey. Embracing the gray is not having a lack of faith or even giving into the enemy. It's acknowledging the reality of what occurs in the life of every human being. Stuff happens, and if we walk throughout life thinking that somehow as Christians we're immune from the effects of the gray, then not only are we in denial, we're also a candidate for spiritual apathy.

But be confident, my friend; as sure as there is the darkness of the night, there's also the promise of the dawn.

"Weeping may last through the night, but joy comes with the morning." (Psalms 30:5)

12

OUR CHAMPION

"A champion is someone who gets up when he can't."

courage

Rocky

— *Jack Dempsey*

Let's be honest: none of us signed up to go through what we've gone through in life. With some people, if they were able to see a video of what they were going to experience throughout the years, in particular with family and health issues, they may have asked the Lord, "Take me now!" But of course no one knows what the future holds; it's designed that way. It's the way it was supposed to be because it's not the good and easy times that define a person's character—'it's the trying and difficult times that do.

It would be nice to be able to walk through life with blue birds chirping overhead, no dark clouds on the horizon and a rainbow of skittles following us wherever we go. But 'it's not life, is it? No, it's more like, "Lord, why is my child on drugs? Why was I not good enough when my spouse had an affair? I keep praying, God, but my health just continues to gets worse. My heart is broken, Lord. Why did the love of my life have to die? I try and try, but I just can't beat this addiction. Why, Lord, did mental illness have to entrap my life?

Will I ever get better? I struggle with my faith, God, because life has fallen on top of me like a mountain. Can I be honest with You in expressing my feelings, or must I be silent? I've served You for many years, Father. I've given You my life, my marriage, my children, and my finances and all seem to be shot to hell now. Where did I go wrong? What happened?"

These and a thousand other questions run through the minds of countless Jesus followers who struggle yet dare not outwardly express their feelings because they live in apprehension that they will be labeled as "having little faith," "having sin in their lives that's causing the problems," or "just not walking close enough with God."

Author Jack Watts said, "*God is interested in us being forthright—not in us being piously pretentious. God loathes hypocrisy—just like most of us do. He definitely understands adversity though, having experienced it through the suffering of His Son. This means God can and does empathize with each of us. This makes Him fully capable of meeting us exactly where we are, regardless of our situation, despite the level of our dysfunction. As difficult as it may seem, He loves each of us exactly the way we are.*"

Our healing begins when we see our pain not as separating us from God but rather connecting us to Him [in the journey] through His great grace and compassionate agape. To not express the anguish of our journey with God is to be disingenuous and therefore not honest with Him. To hold to an absolute that says we are a people of faith who trust in a loving, caring, impartial, compassionate, and grace-filled God and then feel that we can't be transparent with Him regarding our disappointments and questions is in and of itself a form of hypocrisy. We have to get it! He is "*a man of suffering, and familiar with pain [deepest grief].*" Jesus totally understands the magnitude of human emotional pain, grief, and suffering. He knows what it's like to be rejected by family members and by His community, mocked,

We fail to remember christ's torture

lied about, loved and then not loved anymore by the same people, misunderstood, depressed, anxious, sad, tearful, shamed, disgraced, discouraged, questioning God, and tortured. If you receive nothing else from this book, please catch this … that Jesus gets your *pain* and *sorrow.* He really does! He became what you are so that He could "get" what you go through. He feels and understands your human frail condition and because of that He bore that condition for thirty-three years and now is a shareholder with us in our discouragements, hurts, questions, sadness, and pain. He championed over the power of the enemy in our lives with His love gifts to us through His death, burial, and resurrection. As a result we can get up, even when it appears that we can't.

The Need of Being

Listen: life only has true meaning in the struggle. Jesus proved that. Our weaknesses mandate consistent encounters with God and confidence in His love. If not, it might seem as though defeat has wasted our dreams away. He championed over the oppressive thoughts that roll around in our head and says, "God won't come through for us." We have to try and reach beyond the pain, disappointment, and sorrow to the place of where our dreams live with God. Acts 17:28 says, *"For in him we live and move and have our being."* We exist, live, and move by being in Him. Whether that's during a time of confidence or a time of discouragement it is part of my existing (being) with God. I don't have to like it, agree with it, or even understand it. All I need to know is that outside of Him there is no place to move … nowhere to hide. There is no safe shelter that can house my capacity to need God. I love Him, and then I'm angry with Him. I rejoice in His blessings, and I lament when He seems to have forgotten my address. I'm awestruck when I hear His voice clearly, and I cry out in the dark helplessly when He's silent. But it's those *consistent encounters*, those times of *being*, regardless of the circumstances, that help keep the motor running even if I can't understand why.

It's our vulnerability to this present life and it's psychological, physiological, and emotional effects that wreak havoc on our fallen human condition. Outside of us, there is Him. Outside of Him, there is still nothing but Him. That's the reason David said, *"Where can I go from your Spirit? Where can I flee from your presence?"* It's in being with God, whether in good times or in bad times, that we discover who we really are as well as our capacity to endure. There's no escaping His presence, nor is there a time limit to His love and protection, though at times it may feel like He's gone on vacation and has forgotten about us. The hardcore truth is God never promised that everything would go our way and that we wouldn't experience difficulties, heartaches, struggles, or pain in life. Matter of fact, He said quite the opposite.

"I've told you all this so that trusting me, you will be unshakable and assured, deeply at peace. In this godless world you will continue to experience difficulties. But take heart! I've conquered the world." (John 16:33, *The Message*)

Character is birthed out of adversity … but honestly, who wants adversity? Unfortunately, you can't have the one without the other. I didn't want severe facial nerve pain as a result of *trigeminal neuralgia*, but in order to be free of pain, I had to have surgery, "microvascular decompression" at the base of my brain stem. Thank God it worked! But if there were no surgery, there would be ongoing pain. God showed me multiple things about myself through that year of that *hellish* pain and even many years following. I was made aware of several things in me through this adversity that otherwise I would never have known or experienced. What I thought I could never endure, by God's grace I did endure. Where I thought I was alone and abandoned by God, He actually was with me all of the time. When I was fearful, insecure, and traumatized by pain, I found out that He too was familiar with all three of those experiences and was empathetically interceding for me before the Father. There was nowhere else to go. Even in my broken body, like a child in the dark frightened and looking for his daddy, I reached out for His hand to hold on to. Though the voice of pain kept telling me *He's not here to help you*, my desperation to *be* with Him, even through the struggle, was greater than the voice of pain. What I'm saying is He's all we have. He championed our capacity to know Him more intimately and depend on Him more completely, especially through the darkness.

It's interesting… there are 365 verses in the Bible that say, "Fear not." God provided us with one 'fear not' message for every day of the year! Why? If He hadn't, it may seem like He's forgotten about us in the struggle. When we connect with God's beautiful grace and love then we have no need to fear… He's with us, even through the dark places. It's here's where God lives: between weariness and grace, sorrow and gladness, fear and faith, restlessness and peace [being]. His ability in Christ to champion our human equilibrium with Him as we struggle between faith and faithlessness, dependency and independency, love and anger is nothing shy of astonishing!

If ever there was anyone who needed a champion, it was the Israelites. As their army camped in the Valley of Elah, they were held at bay and humiliated daily by the tauntings of the Philistine strongman, Goliath. David, the young confident shepherd son of Jesse, had brought some food to his brothers who were in Saul's army. When David heard that this Goliath Philistine reprobate guy was mocking the Israelites, he became furious and asked permission to go out on the field of battle to fight him. David was totally convinced that the same God who delivered him from the jaws of the lion and bear (1 Sam. 17:34–37) would also give him victory over this arrogant and blasphemous giant. And that's exactly what He did.

David's conquest over Goliath reminds us of the Messiah's victory over Satan. Every one of us was hopelessly enslaved by sin and in desperate need of a champion. Then God sent His Son, His only beloved and cherished Son, Jesus, to deliver us from the grip of death that Satan held on us. Our champion, Jesus, came to earth as a frail man, faced all our human trials, sorrows, and pain (Heb. 2:14–15) and then went into the bowels of hell and fought a very harsh battle on our behalf. This means He has felt what we feel, experienced our same disappointments, understands the depressed, and cries with the brokenhearted. His death and resurrection paved the way to victory in all of those areas and 10,000 times more. It's our Champion, bloody and tattered as He was, who kept getting up when He couldn't, finally striking the enemy to the ground with a death blow.

The prize of this battle being fought between our Champion and Satan was for God's kids, His creative work of unspeakable and matchless amazement… the God-crafted human being. This living, breathing soul who was created in the "image" and "likeness" of God was a representation of what the Omnipotent God and His Son looked like in a human form (Genesis. 1:26). You see, even after the Fall of man, God couldn't stop loving us. It's kind of like when your child is disobedient and you've punished them. As much as you try, you just can't stay angry with them for long. You have to reconnect because you love them that much. Through their flaws, shortcomings, stupid mistakes, unwise decisions, selfishness, still you love them. That doesn't mean there's not consequences for the wrongs, but it does mean that you'll stand by them and support them even through the punishment. But ... just let someone else try to do the punishing or start pushing your kid around or hurting them, that's when the fur flies, the blood boils, and the champion in you comes out to protect and rescue your kid! That's our Father God when it comes to you!

It was our Champion's driving passionate love for us that compelled Him to stand in our place and take the beating for us. We were dead in the water. There was no place to go or hide. Like Goliath, our foe was too big, too powerful, too crafty. We didn't have a chance. He was out to kill us and that meant eternal darkness and separation forever from our Abba Father as a result of Adam's original sin. We're talking totally hopeless here. But with God, what appears to be hopeless is nothing more than a mirage, an illusion of something that just looks bleak. His love will always end up bringing us through the struggle and eventually to a place of safety and being in Him. It may not always happen in the way that we'd prefer or in the timely manner we'd like, but He will appear. Even through the darkest clouds, our Champion will show up with gifts of grace, mercy, courage, vitality, perseverance, endurance, and emotional stability.

The great Hymn "The Love of Christ Is Rich and Free," by William Gadsby, sums up our Champion's finished work for us. The third verse is awesome!

> Love has redeemed His sheep with blood;
> And love will bring them safe to God;
> Love calls them all from death to life;
> And love will finish all their strife.

Peace is not the absence of conflict. It's *knowing* that you're loved through the storm, that you're going to make it. Our Champion gets the fact that life is hard at times, for some even really hard. It's His passionate love and amazing grace that sustains us through the strife and conflict of life. Grace may not always cure your challenging situation in the moment, but it will provide God's loving kindness and His tender affection which will ultimately produce the tenacity you need in the struggle.

A Faithful Defender

When you look at the account of Gideon's life in Judges 6:11–8:32, you see things starting out with the Israelites being ravaged by the Midianites as a direct result of their disobedience to God. For seven years the Israelites experienced invasions from the Midianites, Amalekites, and other Eastern foreigners who ended up ruining their crops and destroying their cattle. Even though they were unfaithful to God by worshipping the gods of the Amorites, still they cried out to God for help. Because of God's great lovingkindness (Psalms. 36:7) He sent them a prophet to once again make them aware of how He provided for them throughout their existence and just how quickly they could forsake Him.

God, as He does with us today, heard their cries and sent an angel to Gideon to commission him for battle. Gideon, whose name means "cutter of trees," belonged to a very common family. There was nothing high and mighty about him. Gideon was willing to go to war against the bad guys, but he just really needed to know that God was speaking to him to go to war. God confirms to Gideon he wants to use him and then reduced his army from 32,000 to 300 men … YIKES! Yet God came through and defeated the Midianites because He heard

His kid's cry out for help. They were crying out to "Him" now, not some stupid, false god. Gideon needed a *defender*, a champion to give them the victory over the thing that was suppressing them, and that's exactly what God did. It didn't happen overnight, but it did happen.

What we learn from Gideon is no matter how great the odds are, no matter how much is seemingly stacked against you, God will defend you and show Himself faithful, sovereign, and strong. It's really only in the struggle that we gain strength to persevere. Isaiah tells us that *"He gives strength to the weary and increases the power of the weak"* (40:29). It's a reciprocal thing. I keep reaching and crying out to Him through my brokenness, and He keeps giving me the ability to sustain the punches with a heavenly power that supersedes my weakness. The help, or the answer to the thing that we're trusting Him for, may not necessarily come in the form or even in the timing that we would like, but for sure He will prove to be our Defender and Champion. It would seem that often in our walk with God, faith sees better in the dark than in the light. Isn't that really the way that faith is supposed to be acted upon? When it really counted, ultimately Gideon needed a defending champion to beat back his enemies for him, and that's exactly what God did, beating the odds of that fight 300 to 135,000!

Championing Our Insecurities

At Whitney Houston's funeral service, actor Kevin Costner touched on a profound subject that many people struggle with...insecurity. Costner said, *"The Whitney I knew, despite her success and worldwide fame, still wondered,* Am I good enough? Am I pretty enough? Will they like me?" The perils of our life journey can take a toll on the way that we see ourselves...our perception of who we are. The sum of what makes us, US, can only be defined through the sacrificial wounds of our selfless Lover…just as we are. If not, then there's no peace. *Good enough* then NEVER becomes good enough no matter who it comes from or how often it's said to us.

In his article, *"The #1 Way to Fight Insecurity,"* Ben Reed, author and small group pastor at Saddleback Community Church in Lake Forest, CA, speaks to how our insecurities are really a way for God to "show off" through us.

Moses is one of my favorite heroes in the Bible, partly because of the danger surrounding the time of his birth, partly because he was an amazing leader, partly because he got to part an entire sea. But mainly he is my hero because I love how *real* Moses appears. You get to see Moses' humanity throughout his story. The fact that he's weak, doubts his call, and messes up gives me loads of hope that God could use me despite my weaknesses, doubts, and failures."

God called Moses to lead the oppressed Israelites to freedom from their bondage to Egypt, and Moses doubted whether this would work. After all, he was just Moses. And Pharaoh was the most powerful man in the world.

In Exodus 4, so God could prove to Moses that He is who He says He is, God asks Moses to throw his shepherd's staff on the ground. When he does, it turns into a snake. He then asks Moses to pick it up by the tail. Not the head, the tail. (For the record, I have some level of faith, but if you ask me to pick up a snake by the tail, I'm out. Call someone else.)

Moses picks it up. Then God tells him to put his hand into his cloak. When Moses pulls his hand out, it's leprous. God instructs Moses to put his hand back in his cloak, and when Moses pulls it out, his hand has returned to normal.

Cool story, no? Crazy miracles, no? Moses had seen two miracles right before his eyes, but still responded with this:

"O Lord, I'm not very good with words. I never have been, and I'm not now, even though you have spoken to me. I get tongue-tied, and my words get tangled."—Exodus 4:10

Sticks turning to snakes. Hands being turned all crazy. *And Moses still doubted?* Doubted that God could use his bumbling mouth to lead a people to freedom? Doubted that God could do what He said He'd do? Doubted God would come through for him?

Yep. Moses listened to the voice of insecurity.

The Critical Inner Us

own worst enemy

upbringing
religion
conflict

So what events in our lives happened that have caused us to come to certain conclusions about us? What's happened in our world that's fostered those insecurities that we carry? *bipolar depression*

The life experiences that we've had with the people who have raised us and consequently influenced us as children tend to be where the root of our insecurities come from as adults. If you've been raised with a parent or guardian saying to you, "You're a dummy," "You're ugly!" then that may be a major reason you say, "I can't ever get this right; I'm just stupid!" or, "I look terrible in this dress; I'm so fat!" Actually, our insecurities don't even have to be verbalized to affect us. A parent's absence can leave a child feeling insecure, and that child then comes to the conclusion that they must have something wrong with them for that parent to not want to be near them. What this does then is build insecurities in the child who ends up building even bigger insecurities as the child grows up into an adult. How do we tame the critical inner us?

Word of God

The best way to calm the critical inner us is to *listen* to what God says about you rather than what has been said to you. God speaks of the very nature of how He feels about you as well as just who you really are in His sight. His champion words regarding you are defended by what He says about you in His Word, the Bible. His words have merit and the power to transform your life and help you to see yourself differently from what you may have been told about you as children.

FIRST: **You're a child of God**

"But to all who believed him and accepted him, he gave the right to become children of God." (John. 1:12, NLT)

SECOND: **You're a friend of Jesus**

"I no longer call you slaves, because a master doesn't confide in his slaves. Now you are my friends, since I have told you everything the Father told me." (John. 15:15, NLT)

THIRD: **You're unconditionally and deeply loved by God**

"Do you think anyone is going to be able to drive a wedge between us and Christ's love for us? There is no way! Not trouble, not hard times, not hatred, not hunger, not homelessness, not bullying threats, not backstabbing, not even the worst sins listed in Scripture." (Romans. 8:35, MSG)

"God showed how much he loved us by sending his one and only Son into the world so that we might have eternal life through him." (1 John. 4:9, NLT)

FOURTH: **God will never condemn you**

"So now there is no condemnation for those who belong to Christ Jesus." (Romans. 8:1, NLT)

FIFTH: **You're totally accepted by Christ**

"Therefore, accept each other just as Christ has accepted you so that God will be given glory." (Romans 15:7)

SIXTH: **You're the righteousness of God in Christ**

"For God made Christ, who never sinned, to be the offering for our sin, so that we could be made right with God through Christ." (2 Corinthians 5:21, NLT)

SEVENTH: **You've been completely set free in Christ**

"So Christ has truly set us free. Now make sure that you stay free, and don't get tied up again in slavery to the law," (Galatians 5:1 NLT).

legalism

EIGHTH: **You're absolutely unique to God**

"And he gives us the power to live, to move, and to be who we are...." (Acts. 17:28, CEV)

The critical inner us can really smack us around through life if we don't allow the words of God, the very essence of what God feels about us, to resonate with our hearts and minds. This is so vitally important to understand as we walk through the difficulties of our struggle to a place of being able to struggle well.

Jesus, Champion of Relationships

Emotional healing is not sustained primarily through just trying to fix someone with psychotherapeutic models of counseling. The foundation of emotional healing is sustained through relationship. The forms and methods of counseling then are built onto this foundation. It's the relationship that supports the tools for healing, not the reverse.

Jesus hung out with all kinds of unsavory characters ... wounded and sick ones, too. Listen to what Jesus said to the Pharisees in Mark 2:15–17 when it comes to all of *us* strugglers.

15 Later, Levi invited Jesus and his disciples to his home as dinner guests, along with many tax collectors and other disreputable sinners. (There were many people of this kind among Jesus' followers.)

16 But when the teachers of religious law who were Pharisees saw him eating with tax collectors and other sinners, they asked his disciples, "Why does he eat with such scum?"

17 When Jesus heard this, he told them, "Healthy people don't need a doctor—sick people do. I have come to call not those who think they are righteous, but those who know they are sinners." egotism + pride get in the way

Jesus relationship with God wanted Him to be x obedient please His faith

Jesus did a number of things that rubbed against the grain of the so-called politically correct of His day. The thing that mattered to Jesus more than anything else was to walk in the will of His Father, go where God wanted Him to go, say what God wanted Him to say, and be with those the Father wanted Him to be with.

Jesus had a true shepherd's heart. His care and love for His sheep was more important than His own reputation, His own safety, and ultimately His own life. He interacted with people, built relationships with them, and out of those relationships healing took place. His words were life, but those words were delivered through the means of relationship. He did this in three ways.

FIRST: Jesus touched people

"Large crowds followed Jesus as he came down the mountainside. Suddenly, a man with leprosy approached him and knelt before him. "Lord," the man said, "if you are willing, you can heal me and make me

clean." Jesus reached out and touched him. "I am willing," he said. "Be healed!" And instantly the leprosy disappeared. (Matthew. 8:1–3)

Look what Jesus did. He stretched out His hand and *touched* the leper. Let's face it, that leper in real-time could have been me, you, or anyone else. Jesus wasn't constrained by the nastiness and disease-ridden body of the leper. That wasn't near enough to stop Him from reaching out in compassion and touching this man. Jesus could care less that the Law said to completely stay away from people with such skin diseases (Lev. 13:45).

Jesus confronted the Law with all of its human shortcomings and then fulfilled it by giving us a *"better covenant"* with God than what the Law had to offer (Hebrew. 7:22).

The Messiah not only touched the leper and healed him, but He touched others in the scripture and did the same thing. From that time until now, He hasn't stopped touching people in their struggle. When He touches us, we touch Him as well, both experiences happening through the Holy Spirit. It's an act of relationship. Our Champion Lover and Defender reaches out to us and deliberately touches our infirmities when it seems that there is no one else or nothing else that can help us. It's that relationship that we build with Him through both struggle and strength that commands our attention. We're then *present* with Him through the struggle, and He with us. That means He's there, available and near and touching us with His hands of healing like a surgeon operating on an unconscious patient. We can't tell the healing is going on, but it's happening. Not all things are immediate with God, but God does all things well.

SECOND: **Jesus looked at people** ~~had~~ *noticed compassion*

Having a conversation with the rich young ruler and trying to get him to see beyond his religiosity, Mark writes in 10:21, "*Looking at the man, Jesus felt genuine love for him.*"

There's something about a person looking you in the eye when you're talking to them that makes you feel important. It lets you know that the person is shutting out the rest of the world and its noise so as to pay special attention to you and what you have to say. It gives you the feeling that you matter to him. That's what Jesus was doing with this young man. Even though the guy had been living in a religion based on works, still he wanted "eternal life," yet could only conceive of it through the religious lens of *doing*. The man was obviously struggling. But rather than rebuke this young man, instead, Jesus *"felt genuine love for him."* Now you have to get the words "genuine love" here (NLT). *Genuine* means authentic, real, original, bona fide, true. *Love* (Agape) means selfless, sacrificial, unconditional, the highest of the four types of love spoken of in the Bible. This is what happened. Jesus looked this kid right in the eyes and before saying one word to him, legitimately, genuinely, and unconditionally loving him with a love that was founded, formed, and flowing straight from heaven. Jesus interacted with the young man through a God-loving connection first. After that He entered into conversation with him to try and get him to break his religious chains and love for money. When he first looked at him, He didn't see the sinner but rather the struggler. He wanted to champion him to a place of self-identification, but the guy couldn't go there. *"He went away sad"* because Jesus' words were too much for him to swallow.

It's the same with us. At first we may not get what Jesus is trying to say to us or do for us, but that doesn't change the fact that He looks us in the eye and makes us feel important and special even if we walk away. His care is genuine. His love is endless. His intentions are to never stop taking us to that place of being *present* with Him until our struggle turns into strength.

THIRD: **Jesus listened to people**

In Luke 24:13–39, we see Jesus on the road to Emmaus with two of His disciples who were on their way to Jerusalem. The men were tired and discouraged. They had followed the Messiah and then saw Him die on the cross. They had no idea that He had risen from the grave.

Jesus just walked up to them on the road and asked them, "What are you guys talking about?" (God had blocked their eyes from recognizing Him). One of the men, Cleopas, said to Jesus, "Are you the only guy around Jerusalem who doesn't know what's been going on these last few days?" Rather than exposing Himself for who He was and filling them in on all of the "updates," Jesus instead asked one question and then just *listened* to Cleopas and the other guy. *"What things?"* "You haven't heard the things said about Jesus of Nazareth, this man who was a prophet, who had mighty powers as well as a mighty word from God for anyone and everyone who would listen to Him? The chief priests and the religious Law keepers delivered him up to the Romans to be condemned to death by crucifixion. But you know what? We all had hoped that He was the one to redeem Israel, but we don't know now … we just don't know." So Jesus just kept listening and listening until finally, when the time was right for them to hear, He then, *"beginning with Moses and all the Prophets,"* filled them in on all of the updates about Himself. (But they still didn't recognize Him.) When they stopped at a village to spend the night, they all sat down at the table. Jesus took some bread, blessed and broke it, and gave it to them. And it was in that moment that

God unblocked their eyes, and they recognized Him as the Messiah. As soon as they did, He was gone.

Jesus could have performed all kinds of miracles and even rocked heaven and earth if He wanted to. But no, He decided to just love these two disciples of His and *listen* to their story. He understood that they were discouraged and disillusioned. He wanted to give them time to "get it out" and express their sorrow. He just wanted to be *present* with these men and care for them with love and undivided attention. They didn't even know that they were *present* with Him until their eyes were opened. Isn't that the way it so often is as we walk with Jesus? He's carefully healing us through the struggle. As we're crying out, at times feeling like He isn't even listening, He really is, and much, much more. *"Didn't our hearts burn within us while he talked to us on the road, while he opened up to us the Scriptures?"* As with the disciples in the Upper Room on the Day of Pentecost, it often happens in our struggles that *"suddenly"* He fills the house. It's only then that we see Him for who He is ... the gracious, powerful, timely, loving God!

13

STRUGGLING WELL

"Great works are performed not by strength but by perseverance."

— Samuel Johnson

As a matter of personal reference, I've come to find out, since walking with Jesus as a newly saved, hippy rock drummer back in 1970, that not everything is so cut and dry in life; yes, even as a Christian. Life's heartbreaking struggles are not as theologically black and white and easy to navigate through as some of our evangelical family may want us to believe. Not everything is so surgically precise or clearly distinguishable throughout our journey with God, and certainly not when you're dealing with raw human emotions. No matter how many prayers you pray or how much you lament and cry out to God, sometimes life just hurts and hurts badly.

The pain of human suffering doesn't come to a screeching halt at a person's door just because they're a believer in Jesus. And for those who have walked with God for some years, surely you know this to be true. Life doesn't always fit neatly into a prepackaged Christian dream of *"God is good all the time; all the time God is good."* Though God in reality is a good God, a loving, just, and gracious God, still that little phrase doesn't always cut it when you feel you're past your last prayer and the salt water of life is now beginning to spill into your nostrils. The word *struggle* itself illustrates a violent effort, a wrestling to get free of something that's restraining or constricting you. Take this and blend it with every word, every belief, every ounce of trust, dedication, and faith that you've invested throughout the years into your Christian walk and then let me know if things mostly have come out smelling like roses and looking like the ending to a family friendly Disney movie. This isn't a slam toward God, not at all! As a matter of fact, it's quite the opposite.

The War of Two Worlds

Jesus was crystal-clear in warning us about the anguish and sorrow that this life can throw on us.

"I have told you these things, so that in me you may have peace. In this world you will have trouble. But take heart! I have overcome the world," (John. 16:33).

We need to understand that Jesus was talking to the disciples here. Yes, they would go through troubles and persecution while preaching the Gospel, but they were His disciples then, and we are His disciples now. Nothing has fundamentally changed there. Jesus is talking about the pressure, anguish, burdens, and troubles that each of us...all of us...will go through here on this huge mass called *earth*. This place started out as a perfect garden of beauty filled with innocence, immortality, and the endless and glorious presence of its Creator, God Himself. There was no trace of burdens or anguish or troubles. They were nonexistent. Probably the only struggle that Adam had was trying to keep his heart from pounding out of his chest when he first laid eyes on Eve! Then the earth was flawless, and so was man. Eden itself was an unspeakably beautiful garden with trees pleasing to the eyes, the tree of life in the middle, God's own irrigation system (a river) watering the garden and four other headwaters with gold running through them. God also formed every kind of wild (yet harmless) animal, bird, and fish straight out of the ground. What a sight it must have been! It was the most AWESOME of all AWESOME places! (Genesis 2:8–20)

But the earth that Genesis 2 speaks of and the earth that Jesus is talking about in John 16 were two very, very different places. Whereas Eden was free of trouble, the earth after the Fall was filled with nothing but trouble. That's why Jesus was warning us about "this world." He was clearly differentiating between the world *before* the Fall and the world *after* the Fall. God's peace inundated every square inch of the world before Adam messed up, but after he messed up God's peace evaporated like a mist on a hot, dry afternoon. In the blink of an eye, Adam and Eve went from innocent obedience to God to a state of guilty disobedience. They went from a place of esteem and peace, to the depths of dishonor and shame. It was that quick and that devastating, for them and for us.

Because of Adam's sin, God went from saying His created world was "very good" (Genesis. 1:31) to a flurry of curses starting with the serpent, to pronouncing pain on Eve, to cursing the very ground that God gave Adam to work (Genesis 3). It's this world, the world that Jesus is telling us that we will have trouble in, that affects each and every one of us, believer and nonbeliever alike. This world has been void of God's peace ever since that dreadful day in the garden. Yet, even through its torment and fury, His celestial peace can still be found. The place to find it is only discovered in the person of Jesus Christ our Savior. Though we all struggle within the debris of this fallen and troubled world, yet sin isn't able to completely keep us from the peace that this world once originally knew. Jesus said, *"In me you may have peace...."* When He said *peace*, He's meaning *tranquility, security, harmony, safety, rest, serenity* and *soul prosperity*. It's His peace, this ray of hope that breaks through the confusion and contradiction of this life's struggle. It's this hope, though seemingly elusive at times, that helps us get up from the *violent wrestling* match that's been trying to pin down every ounce of trust we've put in our faith. It's these two worlds, *pain* and *peace*, that clash together, and the reality of that dichotomous collision can shoot floods of depression and anxiety through anyone. But they must! They have to if we are ever really going to effectively learn to navigate our faith through the highs and lows of this troubled life. Oh, how we wish that it wasn't so ... but it is.

Resolved: *this world will hurt you, but Jesus will heal you of its hurt.* It may not be through a quick miraculous miracle or every loose end of your life being tied up neatly like a red Christmas bow, but it's in that peace, His attainable peace, that place of being in the struggle, that we find the solace to His words ... *"But take heart! I have overcome the world."* That's the payoff of peace through pain. They go together because they live together. Without human emotional pain, we have no true understanding of its antidote, *peace.* And without peace, we have no understanding of what it's like to live outside of pain. But when you place them together and understand better the purpose of each, life tends to then make a little more sense in the struggle.

The struggle is all around us. It landed on earth when Adam fell and exists to this present day. The apostle Paul makes it very clear as to the kind of place we're battling in.

"For we are not fighting against flesh-and-blood enemies, but against evil rulers and authorities of the unseen world, against mighty powers in this dark world, and against evil spirits in the heavenly places," (Ephesians. 6:12).

Now we're talking some kind of evil brawl here! That *evil rulers, unseen, dark world, evil spirits* thing doesn't sound like a walk in the park. That's an emotionally challenging picture of spiritual warfare if I've ever seen one. It's just what it is. It's real, it's ominous, it's intimidating, it's frightening, and it bites. That's the bad news. The good news is we can beat it! Paul goes on to give us the winning ingredient that provides peace and steadfastness for us in the midst of the struggle.

"Therefore, put on every piece of God's armor so you will be able to resist the enemy in the time of evil. Then after the battle you will still be standing firm." (vs. 13)

Without going into all of "the armor," just to say it's all designed to help us withstand the *blasts* that the enemy throws at us in life. Notice that it says the armor is for us "to <u>resist</u> the enemy in the time of evil"... not necessarily <u>overcome</u> the enemy. *Resist* means to *endure, withstand* something that is pressing you. *Overcome* means to *conquer, defeat* the thing that is pressing you. There's a real difference here for us mere mortals to understand when struggling with the evil one. Jesus has completely and thoroughly overcome (conquered/defeated) the enemy as a result of dying on the cross for our sins. That's what He did for us, that's real, that's a fact. Whereas Ephesians 6:14 (NLT) says, *"Stand your ground..."* as you're putting on God's supernatural armor. What we do for Him is to "stand [our] ground." Why? Because we <u>can,</u> that's why! Remember, it's *"Christ IN you, the hope of glory."* (Colossians 1:27) Him being in us (through the power of the Holy Spirit) means we can resist, withstand any punches that the enemy throws at us. That doesn't mean we won't get a black eye, a bloody nose, or even be knocked down from time to time. But it absolutely positively means that he can't "takes us out," he can't ultimately win. The enemy can't beat us for one very supreme reason... because Jesus *overcame* the enemy on the cross. WHOOP, GLORY!! Sorry, I just couldn't help that.

God gives us the stuff to *resist* when the enemy is trying to beat us down. Then, right when you feel he has you down for the count, somehow you notice that you're still *standing firm!* You don't know how, you're not sure why, but you're standing nonetheless. It's God's grace, mercy, love, power and faithfulness that brought you through when you were sure you weren't going to make it through. This is the two worlds that meet in battle everyday of our lives. They tear at one another, the evil against the righteous, the sinister against the good. It's this veil we somehow move through that without fully realizing it, takes us to the other side of pain where the air is a little fresher and our surroundings aren't quite as hostile. It's that place of *being,* that *"peace I leave with you, not as the world gives"* place that Jesus spoke of that has somehow settled in and has taken over where the battle was, even if for just a while.

R.C. Allen said, *"We grow because we struggle, we learn and overcome."* When we find ourselves face-to-face with life's struggles, we have the choice to either totally collapse under its weight and become the victim of its oppression or rise above it to the place where we are *"seated with Christ."* That confident place in each of us where darkness and fear loses its intimidation and influence over us. It's that place of being with Him, a place of peace and mindful tranquility. An area on the battlefield where the enemy isn't allowed to tread a foot on. You feel safe, protected, and loved. Don't try to figure it out. Endless others have tried and it doesn't add up. Then again, 2+2 often doesn't equal four in the Kingdom of God anyway.

The apostle Paul said in 2 Tim. 4:7, *"I have fought the good fight, I have finished the race, I have kept the faith."* Years of struggle failed to crush this man's spirit or evaporate his resolve. Even through the trying times in his life, and there were many, he kept the faith, not perfectly but committedly. Paul came to realize that life was more fragile than it was firm, more surprising than it was steady. But through it all he stayed on the battlefield, and as a result he became tougher at taking punches and more skilled at fighting in war. The battle wouldn't leave him alone, the remnants of the Fall pounded at him every day, and every day he battled back with *"for I know the one in whom I trust, and I am sure that he is able to guard what I have entrusted to him until the day of his return,"* (2 Tim 1:12). That was his hope. That's our hope as well.

When Adam sinned, our ability to neurologically assimilate healthy behavior and keep it retained in the "good box" fell to pieces and became corrupted. Since then we've struggled to be *good,* and all we've gotten in return for our good attempts is a pathetic show of righteousness, which in reality is what Brennan Manning called *"worthless rags."* Here rests the need for a Savior, a Champion who can forgive without first wanting reimbursement, love without first demanding ours, and acceptance without first requiring good deeds. He connects with our struggle and asks that we connect with others in their struggle through what we've learned through the battle. It's our Champion who said, *"Love one another as I have loved you."* Loving each other isn't contingent upon the other person first doing the right thing or living the right *Christian* life before we extend agape to them. It's a love that requires a Divine connection filtered through a broken, dirty vessel that comes out looking like Jesus.

We have to understand that Jesus didn't just come TO us, but He came to be WITH us. With us through our weaknesses, struggles, fears, failures, questions, joys, victories, our getting it right, our getting it wrong, our indecisions and apprehensions, through our highest godly actions, and through our lowest moral failures. Jesus connects and relates with us, and so must we with one another. Jesus doesn't differentiate between dry cleaned and neatly pressed sin and tattered and filthy sin. A cow patty called by any other name is still a cow patty.

Personally I have found in my years of walking with Jesus that pain, in any form, goes hand and hand with our faith walk. Being a follower of Jesus doesn't anymore exempt you from pain and sorrow than being a medical doctor exempts you from getting sick. I've come to realize that the difficulties that all of us go through are just as much a part of our experience with God as our devotion and worship is with Him.

Rick Warren said, *"God never wastes a hurt."* This comes from a man who lost his son to suicide. Yet, Rick and his wife Kay had to walk out the deep pain and sorrow of losing their son through the tears of also knowing that Jesus said, *"You can ask for anything in my name, and I will do it...."* (John 14:13) It's the contrast of the seen and the unseen, the knowing that He can and the disappointment when He doesn't. This is the struggle that both tortures our soul and drives us into the arms of God at the same time. Surely it must have been what David experienced when he said, *"The Lord is close to the broken hearted, he rescues those whose spirits are crushed."* (Psalms 34:18) Or in Psalms 71:20 when David said in his old age,

"Though you have made me see troubles, many and bitter, you will restore my life again; from the depths of the earth you will again bring me up."

It seems like a paradox I know, but encouragingly or sadly, they often meet together in life's struggle, the knowing that He is able, and the disappointment when He's silent. Again, the conflict of knowing that *"The Lord is close to the broken hearted* and *crushed [in]spirit"* and yet not always *feeling* that when it comes to your circumstances. It's the brokenhearted, crushed in spirit stuff that we could do without.

Yet, it's David who said in Psalms 35:9, *"Then I will rejoice in the LORD. I will be glad because he rescues me."* What's really encouraging is that in both chapters (Psalms 34–35), David used the word *"rescues"* in the NLT. Either way, God's going to swoop down and somehow, through some means, rescue us from our distress. He's our *"helper;* [and] *the sustainer of my soul,"* (Psalms 54:4). This is the comfort that the struggling saint has…He watches over our soul and provides peace for us in places where peace shouldn't be. He pushes through the raging battle just to get to us so that He can provide water, nourishment, and bandages to sustain us while in the struggle. Wow, that's love!

Last Word

We're all present and accounted for on this fallen and corrupted planet. We're a motley crew of the standing and the fallen, the confident and the fearful, the victorious and the defeated, the strong and the weak, the faithful and the faithless, the stable and the unsteady. We all make up His glorious crippled church. We're the lovers of Jesus and His Word who will, one day, no longer be subject to the human degradation that has befallen these moral bodies as a result of Satan's death grip. This evil foe can plague our body and mind on this side of heaven, but on the other side, he's utterly powerless! We belong to God, and we've been redeemed from the *curse* because of the Messiah, His Son, Jesus. He paid for our redemption with His unending love and through sacrificing His own body on the cross for us. That means we're FREE from religious Pharisaical legalism and condemnation that somehow makes us feel that we are "less than" in the eyes of God. Well, God has no less than[s], He only has "more than[s]." *"No, in all these things we are more than conquerors through him who loved us."* (Romans 8:37) And though you may not feel like a conqueror in the moment of struggle or even if you've been struggling for a while, nonetheless His promise is that you will, and you will because He loves you, and He won't leave you in that perpetual struggling state. You can rest assured that somehow you're going to breathe again, and it won't be from stale air.

Sin is a systemic problem. It has affected every area of a human's life, and that's a fact. There's nothing that we can do to escape its clutches and there's nothing in and of ourselves that we can do to eliminate it from our lives. But that systemic human disease has been given a powerful antibiotic to fight its deadly sin infested, bacterial infection. That heavenly cure is *Jesus*, the Lover and Protector of our souls.

Alister E. McGrath, professor of Theology, Ministry, and Education at King's College in London, England, said, *"Within each of us exists the image of God, however disfigured and corrupted by sin it may presently be. God is able to recover this mirrored image of Him by virtue of Christ's sacrifice on the cross for us and through the grace that He provides as we are transformed to His reflection."*

There are no limits on His love, and there is nothing that we can do to have Him love us more. He just loves us…period. It took this kind of audacious love to bring out in us the best that can possibly be brought out in any human being. Through all of our weaknesses, mistakes, and personal setbacks in life, still He's there. Like an embedded homing device buried deep within our souls by the Holy Spirit, He calls out to us through our tears to a place of believing that our brokenness and failures won't separate Him from us, and that somehow, just somehow, He'll rescue us from the pressure of our struggles.

Whether I'm standing up, falling down, been right, wrong, weak, or strong, God's passion to love me, through the struggle, is lock-n-loaded for life. He set the world in a new trajectory when He said, in John 13:34–35, *"A new command I give you: Love one another. As I have loved you, so you must love one another. By this everyone will know that you are my disciples, if you love one another."*

That wasn't an optional message that He gave. A person shouldn't have to do something before we decide whether to love them or not. Neither should you have to do something in order for someone else to love you. That's the Jesus style. It was a "commandment" that He not only instructed each of us to do, but He personally lived, breathed, and acted it out Himself here on earth. Why? He is love, that's His very nature, His very being. *"Whoever does not love does not know God, because God is love,"* (1 John 4:8). There are no prerequisites on the Jesus style of love. He doesn't say, "I'll love you if you do something that's worthy of Me loving you." It isn't looking for the good first and then considering rewarding it with love. Admittedly, love isn't easy to extend, in particular if there's been great offense attached to the person you're trying to love. But I do believe it's an ongoing conversation that we should have with God as we're asking Him to increase in our lives as we decrease and take on His *image* as Alister McGrath mentions. Loving the unlovely is also an act of humility. It says, in the end, "I'm no better than you are." It's a ripping through the ugliness of our self-centered deception and coming to the conclusion that all of us are sinners, and ultimately, we're all in the same boat struggling and in need of His grace. If we can get that, then actually, the Jesus style of love is a mirror reflecting back at us, saying, "If you want to be loved through all of your warts, hurts, and shortcomings, then learn to love others who look just like you, who are in the struggle just like you."

In Psalms 136, there's a phrase that's repeated in all twenty-six verses: *"His faithful love endures forever."* (NLT) We really don't know who wrote this particular Psalm, but we do know that it was sung in Solomon's temple and also by the armies of Jehoshaphat when they sang themselves into victory while in the wilderness of Tekoa (2 Chronicles 7:3–2 Chronicles 7:6). Why is this important to us? Life can be, and often is, a weaving in and out of both victories and wilderness experiences. The armies of Jehoshaphat were no strangers to war, nor were they unfamiliar to near-defeat just prior to this battle. Interestingly, King Jehoshaphat appointed *"singers to walk ahead of the army, singing to the Lord and praising him…"* (2 Chronicles 20:21). But the cool thing was what they sang. It just wasn't any old hymn. It was a very specific song that they bellowed out toward their enemy, *"Give thanks to the Lord; his faithful LOVE endures forever."* It's the very same message that's in Psalms 136, and it's that same message that Jesus is trying to get His believers to see today. It's the message that God's beautiful agape love really does endure forever. It endures through our greatest times of joy and happiness and through our worst moments of discouragement and sadness. It's there when we're standing on top of the mountain and when we're struggling to lift the mountain off. It's there in our proud moments of accomplishment, and it's also there in our defeated times of humiliation. The solid truth is this: through the struggle, no matter how we succeed or fail in it, God loves us fervently, passionately, and unconditionally. That's a Biblical, fundamental, bedrock truth, and if we don't get this, life will wear us down to where our hearts become corroded and our earthy endurance is snuffed out.

We struggle, all of us. In some earthly form or in some earthly way, each of us has faced the tempests or will face them. These are the storms of life set in play as a result of Adam's self-centered act of disobedience that rage against these fragile and corrupted jars of clay. But when we do struggle, at least we can confidently know that yes, we struggle, but because of God's great grace and His endless love for us in Christ, we're now *struggling well*.

ABOUT THE AUTHOR

Fred Antonelli, PhD, is founder/director of Life Counseling Center, Inc., with office throughout the Eastern Shore of Maryland and Delaware. He is a Crisis Marriage and Pastoral Counselor and is sought out for his clinical/Christian crisis marriage and pastoral IOP (Intensive Outpatient) therapy.

Dr. Fred has served as a former senior pastor for twenty-three years. He also was host for nine years of the popular nationally syndicated Christian teen and young adult radio show, *Rock Alive*, heard over both the CBN and Salem Radio Network. He has written articles for leading national Christian magazines as well as for numerous independent publications. Dr. Fred is an author as well as a national speaker for conferences, seminars, workshops and pulpit ministry.

Dr. Antonelli is ordained through the Elim Fellowship out of Lima, NY, a Clinically Licensed Pastoral Counselor with the National Christian Counselors Association as well as holding membership with the American Association of Christian Counselors and membership in the American Counseling Association and the International Association of Marriage and Family Counselors. Dr. Fred is also a Board Certified Clinical Sexual Addiction Specialist-Supervisor through the Board of Christian Professional and Pastoral Counselors. Dr. Antonelli holds a BA in Theology, an MA in Clinical

Christian Counseling, and a PhD in Clinical Psychology. He also holds a Mental Health License (LPCMH) with the State of Delaware.

Dr. Fred has been married for forty-five years to his high school sweetheart Debbie, and they have three children and six grandchildren.

★

Bring your sorrows + trade them
for joy

O what a Savior
isn't He Wonderful
Sing Hallejah
fore He is risen!
Bowed down before Him
For He is LORD of all - everyone
including
all of His
creation.
If man doesn't
bow down, in the
Bible, God says even
the rocks will bow
down + speak out

What if we can start over?
What if we can start over?

There's a kind of love
There's a kind of love
. . . that God
only knows!

"Jesus is calling"
Are you hurting
and broken within
overwhelmed by the weight of
Jesus is calling   your sin

Have you come to the end
                    of yourself
do you thirst for the drink
Jesus is calling   of the well

o come to the altar
. God's The father's arms are
                    open wide
forgiveness was bought with
the precious blood of Jesus Christ
Leave behind your regrets + mistakes
come today there's no reason to wait